Gorgeous Paper Gifts

MORE THAN 20 QUICK AND CREATIVE PROJECTS

SUSAN CARROLL & BARBARA E. SWANSON

Bothell, Washington

Credits
Produced by Lark Books, Asheville, N.C.
Project Management: Chris Rich
Design and Production: Theresa Gwynn
Project Acquisition: Kim English
Photography: Evan Bracken (Light Reflections, Hendersonville, N.C.); Richard Jolly-Hasselberg (Jollyhassel Photography, Black Mountain, N.C.)
Photo Styling: Skip Wade
Editorial Assistance: Amy Elizabeth Cook
Illustrations: Megan Kirby

Gorgeous Paper Gifts:
More Than 20 Quick and Creative Projects
©2000 by Susan Carroll and Barbara E. Swanson

All rubber stamps used in this book have trademark registration with the U.S. Copyright Office.

Martingale & Company
P.O. Box 118
Bothell, WA 98041-0118 USA
www.patchwork.com

No part of this product may be reproduced in any form, unless otherwise stated, in which case reproduction is limited to the use of the purchaser. The written instructions, photographs, designs, projects, and patterns are intended for the personal, noncommercial use of the retail purchaser and are under federal copyright laws; they are not to be reproduced by any electronic, mechanical, or other means, including informational storage or retrieval systems, for commercial use.

The information in this book is presented in good faith, but no warranty is given nor results guaranteed. Since Martingale & Company has no control over choice of materials or procedures, the company assumes no responsibility for the use of this information.

Printed in China
by Oceanic Graphic Printing Productions, Ltd.
05 04 03 02 01 00 6 5 4 3 2 1

ISBN 1-56477-312-4

CIP data available upon request

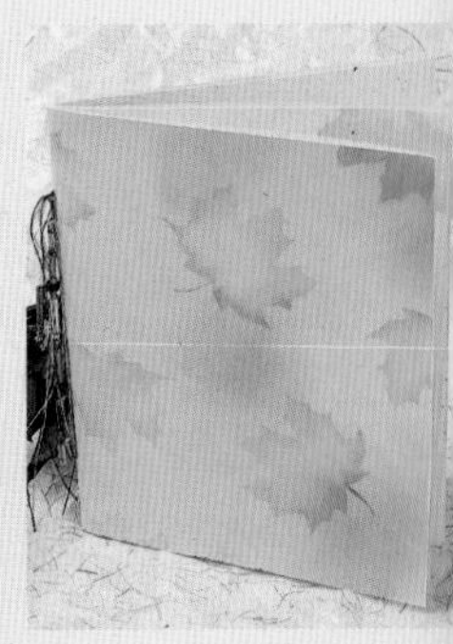

Contents

Introduction

Close your eyes for a moment and imagine a few sheets of ordinary paper. Now envision yourself transforming them into stunning gifts for your friends, for your family—and for yourself. Sound like fun? Or are you worried because you're not an artist or expert crafter? Relax! Even if you've never picked up a rubber stamp, heard of paste paper, or embossed a relief design, with the help of *Gorgeous Paper Gifts*, you'll soon be on your way to creating paper projects as beautiful and useful as any you could find in an expensive gift shop or gallery. Just pour yourself a cup of tea, settle in for a good read, and take your pick from the many carefully selected projects offered here: lovely journals, booklets, and book covers; exquisite ornaments and frames; clocks, desk sets, coasters, gift boxes—and more.

Gorgeous Paper Gifts is divided into two sections: In the first, you'll learn the simple techniques that so many paper crafters already enjoy, including embossing, stamping, paste paper, and stenciling. Each of the first four chapters provides detailed, easy-to-read instructions, "how-to" photographs that will show you exactly what to do, complete descriptions of the required tools and materials, and suggestions as to which papers will work best for each technique. Once you've learned the techniques, you'll be ready to set up your work space and purchase the basic supplies and tools. (Most of these will fit into a kitchen drawer, and they're all readily available at craft, art-supply, and paper stores, and through mail-order catalogs.)

Then comes the best part: picking your first project. In the second section of this book, you'll discover a stunning array of gift items made by creative designers who truly love working with paper—and who know exactly how to do it. Whether you're an old hand at paper crafts or a complete novice, and whether your taste tends toward the traditional or contemporary, you're sure to find projects here to please you. Every one of them comes with a list of the specific materials and any special tools required, so you'll know what to gather before you start. When you're ready to begin, just follow the easy, step-by-step instructions.

Before long, you'll be so comfortable with these paper-craft techniques that you'll be designing and decorating projects of your own. And when your friends and loved ones see what you've made for them, they'll all say the same thing: "Gorgeous!"

Embossing

Run the tips of your fingers over the gracefully raised letters on a wedding announcement or over a textured floral imprint on a greeting card, and you'll be touching the very heart of the technique known as embossing—the art of creating ornamental relief designs on paper. Three different embossing techniques—wet, dry, and heat (or thermal)—are covered in this chapter, so read on and choose your favorite method!

Dry Embossing

Dry embossing is the process of shaping paper by placing it on top of a raised or recessed template and burnishing (or rubbing) it with a round-tipped tool known as a stylus. You don't need much to start—just paper, a stylus, a light source, and a template.

SUPPLIES AND TOOLS FOR DRY EMBOSSING

Many craft, paper, and art-supply stores carry a wide variety of papers suitable for dry embossing. Almost any paper may be dry embossed, but card stock or medium-weight art papers such as watercolor paper produce better results than thinner papers, which may tear, or thicker papers, which may not yield when burnished. The nicer the paper, the nicer the results, so papers with a high rag content are highly desirable. (Rag papers are made with cotton fiber pulp from cotton rags.)

If you're new to embossing, start with white or light-colored papers; they're easy to work with because you can see the embossing templates underneath them. As you become more experienced, you may want to emboss other kinds of papers or different colors of paper.

An embossing stylus, available from many craft stores, is a penlike tool with a ball-shaped tip that's used to burnish surfaces. Stylus tips come in several sizes, and some styluses have a rounded tip at each end: one small tip and one large. Knitting needles, cuticle sticks, chopsticks, and empty ballpoint pens can also serve as burnishers; just make sure the tips aren't too sharp or rough.

Choosing the correct tip size takes a bit of practice. Using a very small tip will help you pick up all the fine design details from your embossing template, but with a small tip, you run a greater risk of tearing the paper as you press it. You'll lessen that risk by using a larger tip, but you'll also sacrifice some of the detail in your design.

Following the outline of a template through opaque paper is much easier when the template and paper are lit from behind. A light box is the ideal piece of equipment for this purpose. The box consists of a simple square or rectangular frame with a sheet of glass or rigid plastic on top and a light inside.

Light boxes are available at art-supply and craft stores, but if you'd rather not purchase one, you can create one instead. Set a sheet of clear or semitransparent, rigid plastic on top of two low stacks of books or wooden blocks. Place a light (fluorescent is best, but any bulb will do) under the structure and—presto!—you have a light box. A glass table with a light beneath it also makes a good substitute for a

1

Raised and recessed embossing templates

commercial light box. In a pinch, you can even hold your embossing project against a sunny window. (Backlighting won't help you emboss the textured surface of a solid object, of course, but it will prove invaluable when you're burnishing the object's outline or the cutouts in a stencil.)

There are two types of embossing templates: raised and recessed (Photo 1). Raised templates are simply thin, firm objects that will raise designs in your paper when you press the paper over them. Recessed templates are objects with designs cut out of them—stencils, for example. You'll press the paper, face down, into the recess to create a raised design on the front of the paper.

Many objects make good raised templates—any thin, solid object with an interesting shape or texture will work, as will thicker objects that have raised relief areas on them. Make sure that the portion of the object over which you plan to emboss is no thicker than 1/8 of an inch. Trying to emboss dry paper over thicker objects is difficult; the thicker the template design area, the more likely the paper will be to tear or fold.

As with raised templates, the hole in a recessed template should be no more than 1/8 of an inch deep when you plan to emboss with dry paper. Plastic quilting templates; drafting templates; and brass and plastic stencils, which come in a variety of patterns, can all serve as recessed templates.

Literally hundreds of items will yield interesting embossed designs, so let your imagination run wild here! Take a look around your home for objects with interesting shapes and textures. Pieces of string or rope that you've arranged to form a design, the textured surfaces of baskets, sections of netting, keys, rings, chains, and unmounted rubber stamps may all be used with this embossing technique. Printing blocks, fiberboard cabinet forms, and linoleum block carvings will also work. Even the contents of your cupboards may be embossing objects in disguise, including rice and beans.

Making your own raised and recessed templates from illustration board (or a similar board) will allow you to draw or trace almost any design you like. You'll find these boards at craft and art-supply stores. Good sources for designs to trace include stencil design books, quilting patterns, and clip art (noncopyrighted images available in books or on computer software). Just make sure you don't violate any copyright laws when you duplicate an existing design!

To create either a raised or recessed template, select a design and trace or draw it onto your board. (A ruler and compass will prove helpful when you're drafting circles, stars, and many other simple shapes.) Next, place the board on a cutting mat and cut out the design with a sharp craft knife (Photo 2, opposite). Cut slowly and carefully, or the rough edges may transfer to your

Tips

- If your stylus catches on the paper as you burnish, rub waxed paper over the stylus tip or the embossing surface to help the tool glide more smoothly. Rubbing the paper gently with your fingertips can help, too; your fingers will leave a very slight residue of oil and moisture on the surface.
- If you have trouble seeing the outline of your pattern, turn down the other lights in the room so your project is entirely backlit during embossing.
- To avoid unsightly sheens on paper that you burnish with its right side up, protect the paper from the stylus by covering it with a layer of tracing paper.

embossed project as ragged outlines. Keep the board from which you cut the design, too: The hole in it can be used as a recessed template.

To add more depth or height to your designs than a single template can provide, stack two or more identical templates with their edges aligned. To create multilevel, stepped designs, stack two or more templates unevenly to create tiered edges. Before embossing the stacked templates, glue the layers together and then glue the stack to a piece of illustration board. Both homemade and purchased templates may be stacked.

DRY EMBOSSING WITH A RECESSED TEMPLATE

To use a recessed template, first place the paper (face up) on your work surface. Then set the template on the paper, with its recess face down and the image positioned as you'd like it to appear on your paper. Attach the template to the paper with removable tape to keep it from slipping as you burnish it. (You'll be glad you did, as it's very difficult to reposition the paper exactly if it slips.) Although artist's tape is best (it's only slightly adhesive), masking tape will also work if you stick it onto some fabric a couple of times to loosen its grip.

Next, place the paper, template side down, onto your work surface or light box. Then, using your stylus, burnish the paper against the inner edges of the recessed template design, gently but firmly pressing the paper into the outline's shape (Photo 3). Work only around the edges of the design; you don't need to burnish the paper in the center of the recess. When you're finished, turn the paper over and remove the tape and template to reveal the embossed design.

DRY EMBOSSING WITH A RAISED TEMPLATE

When you emboss with a raised template, what you see is what you get! After embossing, the raised portion of the paper will look just like the raised portion of the template.

To begin, you may want to glue the template to a large piece of illustration board so that the template will remain stable as you work. Alternatively, you may affix the template to your work surface by attaching double-sided tape to its bottom. Place the paper, right side up, on top of the template and secure it to the board or work surface with removable tape. Next, use your finger to press the paper gently against the template. Then use your stylus to push the paper down more firmly around the template until the raised design in the paper is clear (Photo 4). When you're finished, remove the paper from the template.

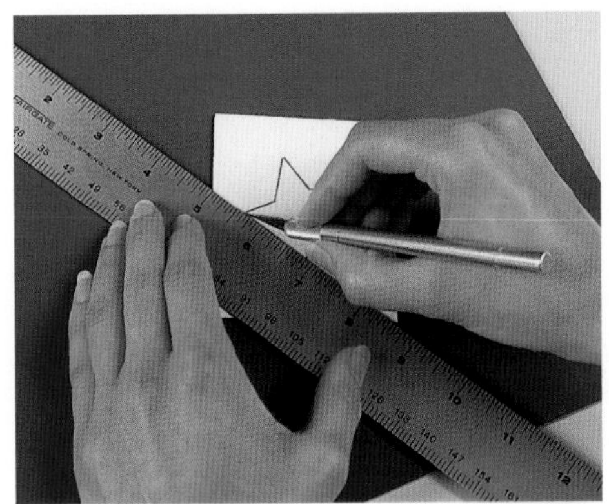

2

Making your own embossing template

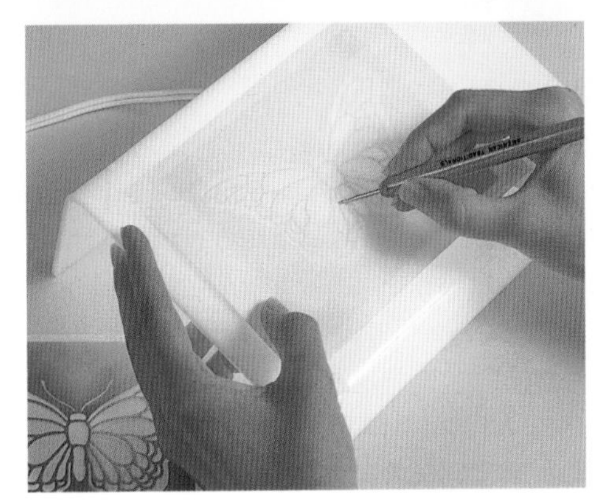

3

Using a stylus to press paper into a recessed template

4

Burnishing around a raised template

Wet Embossing

Papermakers emboss relief designs in their freshly made, still moist paper sheets, but you don't have to be a papermaker to enjoy this process. Instead, you can dampen dry paper in order to shape it. One advantage to wet embossing is that thicker templates may be used, as dampened paper is more flexible than dry paper.

SUPPLIES AND TOOLS FOR WET EMBOSSING

Heavy, uncoated, absorbent papers are best for wet embossing. Many embossers prefer handmade papers because their fibers are less compressed than those of manufactured papers, making them easier to manipulate. Commercial art papers and blotting paper are also good choices. Select papers with a high rag content whenever you can, as their fibers bend easily. For dramatic, deep impressions, use papers that are thick.

One way to wet emboss paper is to place dampened paper on top of an embossing template, cover the paper with a cushioning material, and then press the paper and object between two rigid pressing boards that are weighted down or clamped together. Although some embossers use commercial book, paper, or flower presses for this purpose, it's easy to make your own press instead. You'll need a couple of pressing boards, some cushioning, and a few heavy weights or several C-clamps.

Sheets of rigid plastic and waterproof laminated boards make good pressing boards. Wooden boards will also work if you waterproof them by spraying them with a sealer or by covering them with plastic wrap before using them. A thick piece of felt made of acrylic or polyester fiber or a smooth, thick blanket can serve as a cushion, but make sure that the cushion won't bleed any color when it's damp, or the color will stain the paper. Gather some large books, canned goods, rocks, or bricks to use as weights; or get some small C-clamps, which are available from home-improvement centers and hardware stores. Also have a stylus, a spray bottle or a water-filled tray, and some cheesecloth or a sponge on hand.

WET EMBOSSING WITH A PRESS

The technique itself is quite simple. Start by setting one or more raised or recessed templates on top of one pressing board (Photo 5, opposite). If you're using more than one template, arrange the templates on the board to create an overall design that pleases you.

Next, you must dampen (not soak) your paper. Set the paper on a flat, waterproof surface such as a kitchen counter. Then spritz the paper with a water-filled plant sprayer or brush water on with a wide paintbrush. Patting the paper with a moist sponge or wadded piece of dampened cheesecloth, or quickly dipping both sides of the sheet into a shallow water-filled tray, will also work.

Place the moistened paper, face side up, on top of the template (Photo 6, opposite). At this stage, if your template is very intricate in design, you may want to use a small, wadded piece of dampened cheesecloth to press the damp paper into the design's nooks and crannies.

Next, cover the paper with the colorfast felt or blanket (Photo 7, opposite). You may want to dampen the cushioning material first so that it will further moisten the paper beneath it. (The cushioning material must be smooth, or

Tips

- If your template is made from a porous material such as terra-cotta or an open-grained wood, spray it with a waterproof sealant to prevent the paper from sticking to it.
- Embossing templates sometimes leach their color into the wet paper, providing a welcome surprise or even an intended result. If you don't like surprises, *test press* with a small piece of paper before you start your actual embossing project.

your paper will be embossed with a wrinkled fabric design!) Then position the second pressing board on top of the cushion. Arrange your weights evenly across its top, or tighten the C-clamps around the edges of the two boards, taking care to position them so that they'll apply even pressure around the edges.

Allow the paper and cushioning material to dry. This can take a day or so, depending on the humidity and the thickness and moistness of the paper. When the materials are dry to the touch, carefully remove the cushion and gently separate the paper from the embossing templates with your fingers.

5 Setting the templates on a pressing board

6 Placing moistened paper on top of the templates

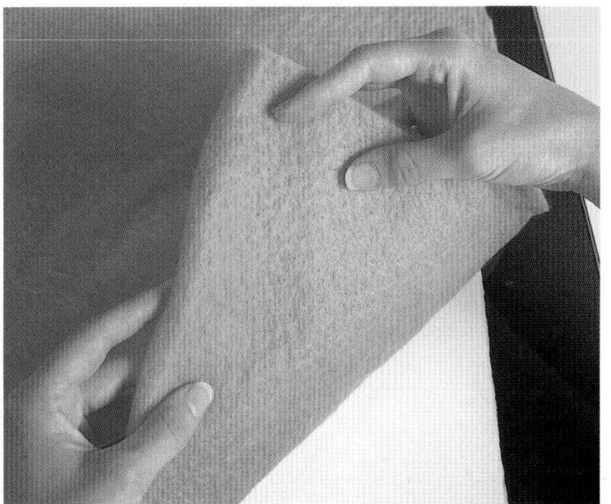

7 Covering the paper with colorfast felt

WET EMBOSSING BY HAND

Many papermakers press their fresh, damp paper by hand, and you can do the same thing with your dampened paper. Either use a wad of moistened cheesecloth to press the dampened paper, or burnish the paper with a stylus. Thicker papers that aren't suitable for dry embossing work very well with this technique.

Gather two towels and spread one of them out on a flat surface. Next, quickly dip each side of a sheet of paper into a tray of water and place the paper on the flat towel. Gently pat the paper with the second towel to remove any excess moisture. Then place the paper over your template and either press the paper into shape with cheesecloth or use your stylus to shape it, just as you would if you were dry embossing. To reduce the risk of tearing your paper, burnish carefully and use only sturdy paper.

Heat (or Thermal) Embossing

Many crafters, including stampers and stencilers, use this technique—which is quite different from dry and wet embossing—to dress up their paper projects. In heat embossing, the surface of the paper remains flat rather than being raised or recessed. Instead, embossing powder is applied to a tacky substance such as an ink and is then melted with a heat gun to create a raised design.

SUPPLIES AND TOOLS FOR HEAT EMBOSSING

Almost any paper can be heat embossed, including coated papers, vellum, card stock, parchment, mulberry, and kraft. You'll need embossing powder, of course; it's the substance that actually melts to produce the raised designs. Clear, colored, iridescent, pearlescent, metallic, and glitter embossing powders are all available.

A variety of slow-drying, tacky substances may be used to create the design itself; they're described in the list that follows:

- **Embossing inks** are made specifically for heat embossing; because they dry very slowly, they remain tacky enough to hold the embossing powder in place as heat is applied to the design. These inks are usually clear or lightly tinted. They're sold in pads and in bottles that are used to replenish dry pads.

- **Embossing pens**, which come not only in clear but in an array of colors, are ideal for adding flourishes to your designs.

- **Slow-drying pigment and fabric inks** are often used by stampers and stencilers, who like to emboss their designs. The inks are first applied with stamps or through stencils and then sprinkled with embossing powder and heated.

- **Condensed oil cremes** (paints that come in stick, crayon, and pot form), which stencilers use to color their designs, may also be heat embossed, as they stay moist and tacky enough to grip the embossing powder that's sprinkled on them.

- **Glue pens** are also good for heat embossing. These come in a variety of nibs and widths and can be used to draw designs. For instance, you might decorate a card by adding some designs with a glue pen, sprinkling the glue with embossing powder, and then heating the powder.

The craft heat guns with which embossing powders are melted look a lot like hair dryers and are available with and without holders. Hair dryers are no substitute for craft heat guns, however. The guns emit more concentrated heat, and the draft they produce is minimal, so they're much less likely to blow the embossing powder off the paper. When you shop for a heat gun, buy one that's designed for use in creating arts and crafts. Hotter guns, used to set epoxies or to heat special paints, for example, may burn your paper. You may have heard or read that irons, electric heating elements, and similar household appliances can be substituted for craft heat guns. Please don't use them; they're harder to control and can be dangerous when they're not used properly.

When it comes to colors and powders, you can mix and match as you like. Colored powders are usually applied over clear inks, and translucent powders are typically sprinkled over colored inks, but experimentation is half the fun in any artistic endeavor. Gold embossing powder over red or green pigment, for example, will yield a rich, gilded effect. And don't hesitate to color a design with more than one embossing powder. Sprinkle powders side by side or emboss one layer of powder before adding a layer of a different color. Keep in mind that metallic embossing powders will often appear a little brighter in your finished project than they look when they're still in the jar. Gold embossing powder, for example, looks a bit brown in the jar—almost antiqued. After heating, however, it turns to a shiny yellow-gold. (Powder colors are usually much shinier after heating.)

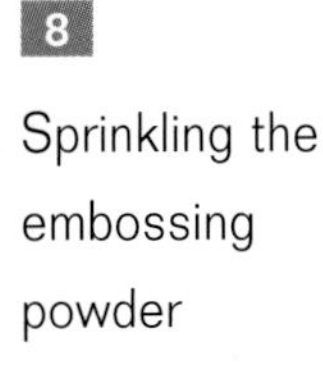

8

Sprinkling the embossing powder

9

Heating the embossing powder

THE PROCESS OF HEAT EMBOSSING

Begin by drawing, stenciling, or stamping a design on your paper, using an embossing ink or pen, pigment ink, fabric ink, condensed oil creme, or glue pen. Next, sprinkle a little embossing powder over the moist design (Photo 8). Gently lift up the paper and tap the excess powder onto a clean sheet of paper. Then lift the clean paper up and use it to transfer the powder back into its container. With a small, dry paintbrush, remove any excess powder that remains around the powder-covered design.

The next step is to apply heat to the powder-covered design. Turn on the heat gun and, holding it about one inch above the design (leave the paper lying on a clean, flat surface), make repeated circular motions over the design to heat the image evenly (Photo 9). Twenty to thirty seconds should be enough time to melt the powder without scorching the paper. As soon as the image has become shiny, remove the heat gun and turn it off, putting it back in its holder if it has one or setting it aside. (Unlike an iron, the gun will cool quickly after you it shut off.) Let the paper and design surfaces cool before you touch them.

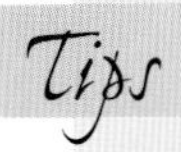

- If you miss a spot during embossing and are left with a tiny flat area where an embossed image should be, re-ink that area using an erasable ballpoint pen. Then sprinkle some powder over the ink, shake off the excess powder, and apply heat. The tips of ballpoint pens are small enough to ink tight areas, and the ink stays moist long enough to grip the embossing powder.
- Emboss the embossing! Using a stencil and stylus, dry emboss a sheet of paper. Leave the stencil in place, and add color to the raised design using one of the suggested media. Remove the stencil and sprinkle the design with embossing powder. Shake off the excess powder and apply heat, melting the powder to add more dimension to the raised design.

Stamping

If you've never tried stamping before, you'll be delighted by the wide range of possibilities that this craft offers. With the simplest of tools and supplies, it's possible to transform even the plainest of papers into beautiful materials decorated with an amazing array of designs. From exquisitely simple to astoundingly elegant, each sheet of stamped paper is as unique as the person who creates it. The first step for beginners, of course, is to become acquainted with the variety of stamps, inks, and papers that are available.

Art Stamps

Craft stores, art-supply houses, and many other shops sell a wide variety of art stamps, which usually consist of three parts:

- **The die** is the portion that contains the image to be inked and stamped. The image may be outlined or solid, and the die may be made of rubber, foam, or clear polymer.

- **The mount (or block)**, which serves as the stamp's handle, can be made of wood, thick foam, or clear acrylic. Usually, wood mounts are trimmed and assembled by hand, and their hardwood construction makes them more durable and easier to grip than less rigid stamps. Stamps with clear acrylic mounts feature clear polymer dies, making images easier to position precisely because you can see them as they will appear on the page. Some blocks have more than one die, each permanently mounted onto a separate surface of the mount. Other blocks share removable dies, which are attached to the blocks with magnets or interlocking cloth tape.

- **The cushion** is the portion between the die and the mount. Not all stamps have cushions. (When working with cushionless, rigid acrylic stamps, place a magazine under your paper to provide some resilience.)

You may buy stamp dies, blocks, and cushions separately, and mount or remount stamps yourself. Specialty stamps are also available, including stamps for creating frames and stamps mounted on rollers, which produce a continuous series of images and are good for creating backgrounds.

CARING FOR STAMPS

Clean your stamp between each inking, to avoid contaminating your colored ink pads and to ensure that the stamped images will be clear. Either wipe the stamp with a damp paper towel or blot it on moistened paper towels. Then use commercial stamp-cleaning solutions, baby wipes, premoistened towelettes, water and dish soap, or other mild cleansers. Avoid any substances that contain ammonia or alcohol, as they can damage rubber. Try to avoid immersing stamps, too; doing so may loosen the mounts. Also, store your stamps away from heat or sunlight to prevent the rubber from becoming brittle.

COPYRIGHTS

One important reminder: The artists who design commercial stamps deserve our respect. Their work is almost always copyrighted, so if you intend to sell any projects you make with their stamps, you must obtain their permission first.

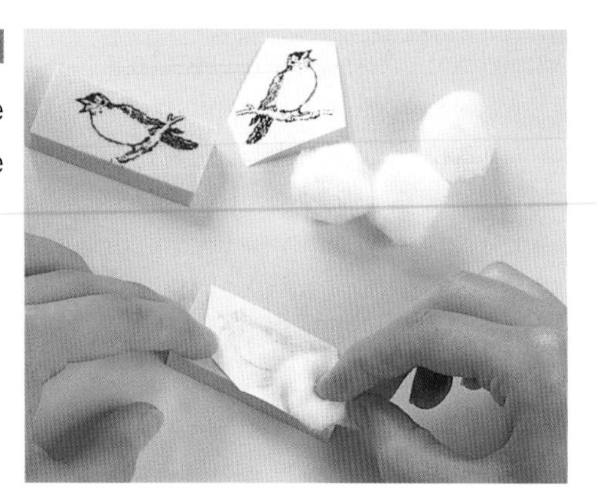

1 Transferring the image

2 Carving the stamp

Hand-Carved Stamps

A fun and inexpensive way to expand your collection of images is to carve your own stamps out of erasers, corks, sponges, linoleum, and other materials. While rubber erasers (including pencil erasers for small shapes) work, many stampers recommend the white, semihard, plastic erasers because they're easier to carve. Household sponges and the dense sponges such as those used for applying makeup work well, too. No matter what material you carve, keep in mind that the image will be reversed when it's stamped.

For hand carving, you'll need scissors and a craft knife or linoleum-block cutters. If you don't want to draw your own designs, just buy clip art. Make a template of the design by using a felt-tip pen to trace the design onto thin cardboard; then cut out the cardboard design. Hold the cardboard firmly onto your stamp material and trace its shape onto the stamping surface with a felt-tip pen.

To transfer an image without a template (this works well with erasers), place a photocopy or laser-printer image face down on your stamping surface. Then rub the back of the image with a cotton swab or cotton ball dampened with nail-polish remover (Photo 1). Lift away and discard the paper. You'll find that the image is now on the eraser.

Scissors are best for cutting solid designs from a sponge. For carving erasers or similar substances, cut around the traced image with a craft knife to create a relief design (Photo 2). As you cut, keep the blade of the knife perpendicular to the surface of the eraser.

Inks and Pads

Five kinds of ink are common in stamping: dye, permanent, embossing, pigment, and fabric. These typically come in felt or foam pads—either rectangular, single-color ink pads or smaller single-color pads about one inch square. Some inks also come in rainbow pads that feature several colors side by side. (One important tip: Store rainbow pads flat; if you set them on their sides, their colors may bleed!) To replenish spent pads or to mix colors on uninked pads, you'll use what are known as re-inking bottles.

- **Dye inks**, which are usually water-based, come in a wide range of intense colors and are best for creating vivid images on glossy paper. They dry very quickly, so they aren't useful for heat embossing. The inks will fade in time, especially when exposed to light.

- **Permanent inks** are waterproof and are perfect for creating stamped images over which you intend to apply water-based media; the images won't bleed or smear when they get wet.

- **Embossing inks and powders** add texture and color to a stamped image. Made for heat embossing, the slow-drying inks are usually clear or lightly tinted, and the powders come in clear, colors, iridescents, metallics, pearlescents, and glitters.

- **Pigment inks**, which are thick and opaque, come in many colors and metallics. Because they dry slowly, these inks are great for heat embossing. In fact, you'll usually have to set them with heat in order to dry them, especially if you use them on coated papers. Pigment inks resist fading.

- **Fabric inks**, although they're designed for use on cloth, also work on paper. Because they're thick and slow to dry, they're good for heat embossing.

Some stampers like to ink their stamps with water-based markers, which are available in many colors and nib widths. Markers are handy when you want to brighten up a stamp that lacks detail; use several markers to ink various colors onto different areas of the stamp. Markers help to highlight intricate designs on an outline stamp.

Paints formulated specifically for stamping have been developed in recent years and come in many colors. These opaque, water-based acrylics work best with bold, simple images. In fact, they're designed to be used with broad-surfaced foam stamps. You may coat your stamps with other acrylics or with tube watercolors, but these, too, should be reserved for solid images. Turn to your inks and markers for detailed designs.

Papers for Stamping

The paper you choose will depend on your project and the effects you want to create. Also, because certain inks are better suited to some papers than to others, the paper you choose may determine the ink you select. Generally, smooth papers work best for stamping because they render crisp images, but feel free to experiment. For a bumpy, gnarled look, a highly textured handmade paper may be just the ticket.

COATED PAPERS

Coated papers—glossy, matte, or dull—all have nonabsorbent surfaces. Because inks aren't absorbed by these papers, stamped images on them are sharp and bright. (Dye inks look especially vivid on white glossy paper.) Coated papers are also perfect for heat embossing because inks dry very slowly on their surfaces. On glossy coated stock, pigment inks won't dry *unless* they're set with heat, so if you don't want to emboss your stamped design, you may want to use quick-drying dye inks and water-based markers instead.

UNCOATED PAPERS (MANUFACTURED)

Uncoated, manufactured stock (plain bond paper included) is absorbent, and inks dry quickly on it. Dye inks and water-based markers work on these papers, but because these inks are absorbed, they appear duller than on coated stock. Thick pigment inks, on the other hand, sit on the surface of uncoated paper and produce rich, vibrant colors.

won't sink into the paper, so they'll hold a sharper image than inks that are absorbed. To make handmade papers less absorbent, just mist them with household spray starch, or make your own solution by mixing ½ teaspoon of powdered laundry starch and 1 pint of water. To dry the sized paper, cover it with a piece of kraft paper and iron it lightly.

OTHER PAPERS

Heavier stocks are often the best choices for stamped cards, bookmarks, and similar projects. Many print shops carry these stocks in the form of blank business cards (great as stamped gift tags), blank greeting cards with deckle edges, and paper in a variety of other shapes. Lightweight papers are especially appropriate as gift wraps or accents. Even tissue paper and paper lace can be stamped. You'll want to avoid typing paper, however, especially the erasable kind; stamped images on it are likely to smear.

And the list doesn't end here! Virtually any paper can be used to enhance a stamped project, including origami, mulberry, and kraft papers. Even if you don't want to stamp their surfaces, you may want to use them as accents or background layers.

VELLUM AND ARCHIVAL PAPERS

Vellum, with its elegant translucence and sheen, comes in many beautiful colors and weights. Because vellum isn't absorbent, inks take a long time to dry on it—a characteristic that makes vellum a good choice for heat embossing.

Papers with a high acid content become brittle with age. Archival papers, on the other hand, are acid-free and should last for at least one hundred years. If you're incorporating photos into your design or would like to create an heirloom project that your grandchildren will treasure, by all means use an archival paper. Fade-resistant pigment inks are a good match here, but make sure you choose pigment inks that are also acid-free.

COLORED PAPERS

Stamped images tend to show up better on neutral or pale surfaces, but once in a while, you may want to choose a brightly colored or dark paper for a special effect. If you do, use an ink that's much darker or much lighter than the paper. Dark or vividly colored papers also make great backdrops for metallic, neon, or other contrasting inks or embossing powders. (Construction paper is fine for practice and for use by children, but it fades and deteriorates quickly.)

HANDMADE PAPERS

Because handmade papers are more absorbent and have looser fibers than manufactured papers, it's best to use pigment inks on them. These thicker, more opaque inks

Your Stamping Workshop

A hard, flat, clean work surface will help ensure high-quality stamped projects, and a pad of blank newsprint makes a fine work-surface covering. Use the pad as scratch paper to test your designs and as a blotter to absorb splatters. When a sheet is dirty, just tear it off and throw it away. Remember, that's blank newsprint stock—not used newspapers, with ink that can rub off and ruin your projects. Make sure you have adequate lighting. Good ventilation is a must, especially if you use substances that contain solvents. (Nail-polish remover and some inks fall into this category.)

GETTING STARTED

Stamping isn't difficult, but the helpful information in this section will make it even easier.

INKING THE STAMP

The traditional inking method—pressing the stamp down onto a large ink pad—requires a certain finesse. You'll want to apply enough pressure to cover the entire stamp surface with ink, of course, but if you over-ink the stamp, the image may blur or smear. (Keep in mind that felt ink pads are firmer than foam pads; you'll need to apply a bit more pressure to the stamp.)

Sometimes, the stamp you want to use is larger than the ink pad. If the pad is raised above the edges of its container, tap different areas of the stamp onto the surface of the pad until the stamp is fully inked. Small pads are designed to be patted on top of stamps (Photo 3), but larger pads with raised edges can be used in this way, too.

You'll find that some rainbow pads have gaps between the different colors in them; these prevent the colors from bleeding into one another. To avoid gaps in your stamped imprint, move your stamp slightly back and forth over the pad to blend the colors' edges on the stamp. To create your own rainbow effects, color your stamps with markers (Photo 4).

POSITIONING THE STAMP

Many people eyeball their stamp placement, but others prefer to use a stamp-positioning tool, especially when they want to make stamped borders meet at right angles or when they want to position a stamp perfectly to restamp an image that came out too light the first time. A stamp-positioning tool provides a 90-degree corner into which the corner of a stamp can be fit. The tools are usually made from a clear material so you can see exactly where to place the stamp. Some tools also feature grids.

To use the tool, first fit it around one corner of the clear plastic sheet that comes with it. (If a plastic sheet wasn't provided with your positioning tool, just substitute a square-cornered sheet of tracing paper that's slightly larger than the stamped image will be.) Next, ink and stamp your image onto the plastic sheet (or tracing paper), making sure that you fit the stamp snugly into the corner of the tool (Photo 5). Then remove the tool and position the stamped plastic sheet (or tracing paper) on the paper you plan to stamp, exactly where you'd like the stamped image to appear.

Fit the tool back around the corner of the plastic sheet. Holding the tool firmly down on the paper, remove the

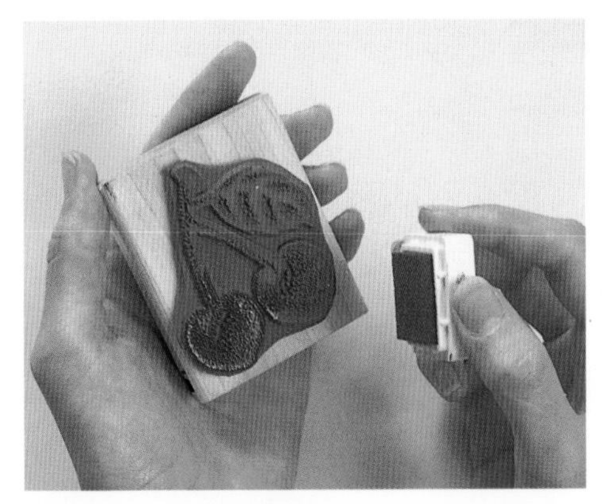

3
Inking with a small pad

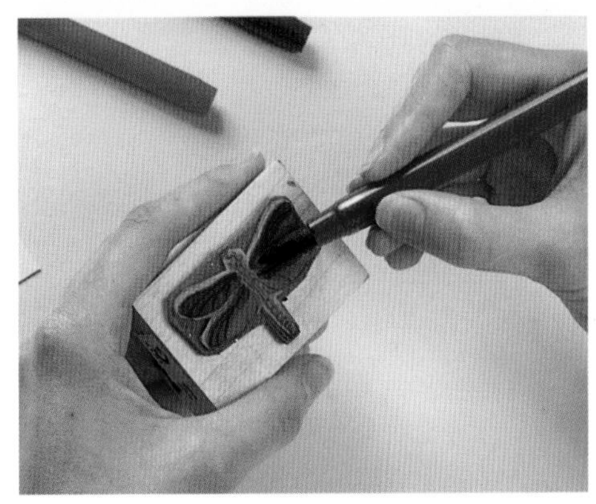

4
Inking with markers

5
Stamping the plastic sheet that comes with the stamp-positioning tool

6 Removing the plastic sheet

7 Stamping the image on paper

stamped plastic sheet (Photo 6). Then stamp your image on the paper, once again fitting the stamp right into the corner of the tool (Photo 7). The stamped image should be precisely where you want it.

STAMPING THE IMAGE

To get a crisp, clear image, apply firm pressure to your stamp. Rocking the stamp or exerting too much pressure as you print can blur the image. After imprinting, raise the stamp straight up while holding down the paper to prevent smears. Then let the ink dry.

Advanced Stamping Techniques

The keys to making lovely stamped projects are learning how to combine basic stamping with more advanced techniques and plenty of practice.

MASKING THE IMAGE

Masking is a technique that's used to create visual depth with repeating or overlapping images. First, stamp the image that you'd like to have appear in the foreground. Next, stamp the same image on a piece of scrap paper—this becomes the mask. (Some stampers like to use sticky notes instead of scrap paper, because the notes' self-adhesive backing helps keep them in place.) Use small, sharp scissors or a craft knife to cut out the mask image (Photo 8, opposite). Then align the mask exactly on top of the original stamped design.

Now stamp the second image, so that part of the ink is deposited on the mask and part on the project (Photo 9, opposite). When you lift the stamp and remove the mask, the stamped image that was protected by the mask will appear to be in front of the second image.

Use a mask, too, when you want to print only one portion of the image on an individual stamp. Let's say you have a stamp of two cherries, but you want to print only one. Stamp the full image onto a piece of scrap paper or a sticky note. Next, cut off and discard the part of the image you want to include in your stamped project. Keep the part of the image that contains the unwanted cherry. Ink your stamp, then cover the unwanted cherry on it with the mask, and stamp the project paper. The mask will prevent the ink from printing the part of the image you don't want.

REPEATING THE IMAGE

Patterned repeats, which are very common in border designs, feature images that are stamped again and again

Tips

- Get two stamps for the price of one by using a marker to ink only one portion of the stamp for one project—and another portion for another project.
- To get more than one imprint from a stamp that you've inked with markers, breathe onto the stamp to remoisten the ink.

in a series, either in rows or in other groupings (Photo 10). In a square repeat, each stamped image lines up with the image next to it, both vertically and horizontally. In half-drop repeats, every other row of repeating images starts halfway down the length or width of the adjacent row. Random repeats are much more subtle; one or more images are stamped repeatedly on the paper, but not in a structured pattern.

CREATING MOTION

To lend a sense of slow motion to your stamp art, try "fading out." Stamp an image on your piece of paper and then, without re-inking, stamp away from the image two or three times, overlapping the imprints if you like (Photo 11). Each image will be paler as it recedes into the background. If you want to keep the original image crisp and sharp, mask it first.

To make an image that seems to move forward very quickly, drag your stamp backward from the stamped image. To keep the initial stamped image clean and free of smears, raise the front of the stamp slightly and drag only the back end (Photo 11). To create a streaked imprint that will make the movement seem faster, drag the entire stamp surface. Practice these techniques on scrap paper until you feel confident with them.

COLORING STAMPED IMAGES

Stampers often color their stamped designs with various media, including pens and markers, colored pencils, pastels and chalks, watercolors, acrylic paints, powdered pigments, and glitter. For descriptions of how these media are used, turn to page 33.

EMBOSSING STAMPED IMAGES

To duplicate the elegant relief designs that you've seen on business cards, stationery, and greetings cards, use the heat embossing technique described on pages 11–13.

8 Cutting the mask

9 Using the mask

10 Repeating images

11 Creating motion

Paste Paper

What fun! Children and grownups alike get to create decorative patterns on paper by running their fingers and a host of implements through colorful wet paste. But paste paper isn't just kid stuff. It has an impressive past as an art form and continues to inspire serious artistic expression in adults.

Paste-Paper Basics

Paste paper is simply paper that has been decorated with one or more colored pastes. All you do to make it is prepare a wet paste, add color to it, spread it over paper, and then create decorative patterns on the paper by pulling tools (including your fingers) across the wet paste or by pressing objects into it. The tools or printing objects create an almost three-dimensional effect by displacing the paste to reveal the underlying paper and its color. Once the paper has dried, it's remarkably flexible.

SUPPLIES AND TOOLS FOR PASTE PAPER

The best papers to use are strong ones that can withstand having tools dragged across them while they're wet. (Highly absorbent papers may shred under such circumstances, and some papers stretch when they're wet.) Good choices include charcoal paper and other medium-weight drawing papers; heavyweight watercolor paper; classic laid text paper; medium-weight bond paper; wove paper (which has a smooth, even surface); and photocopier paper (as long as it isn't too absorbent). Try a variety of paper colors, including black, as contrasts to your colored pastes.

Almost any implement that will leave interesting striations or impressions in the paste is suitable for use as a patterning tool. Your house is probably filled with such tools.

You can press images into the paste with a number of objects. Rubber stamps, burlap, crumpled paper or food wraps, carved erasers, and cookie cutters leave interesting imprints. Carved corks, buttons, bottle caps, the outer rings of plastic cups, carved linoleum blocks, shapes cut from wood, and carved potatoes will also work well. For repeat patterns, carve designs on the surface of a rubber brayer or glue shapes onto it. String wrapped around a brayer also provides interesting effects.

To pull a design across the paste, try hair combs, calligraphy pens, the tines of plastic forks, wood-graining combs, pastry wheels, plastic credit cards, rubber wedge tools, sticks, plastic spackling knives, or old beaded necklaces. Turn stiff plastic or cardboard—or even weather stripping—into combs by cutting serrated edges with a craft knife or scissors. (Cover cardboard combs with acrylic paint to make them waterproof and therefore reusable.) And don't forget the "handiest" tools in your house—your fingers!

To prepare the paste, you'll need a stove, a measuring cup and spoons, a large saucepan and mixing bowl, a handheld electric mixer or a fork, and some resealable plastic food containers or glass jars to hold the finished paste. (You may need a blender, too, if your paste is lumpy.)

To color the paste, you'll mix a water-based coloring agent into it. Any one of the following agents will work: powdered or liquid tempera; natural pigment; batik dye; or

tube gouache, watercolor, or acrylic paint (including metallic and pearlescent). Make sure you have containers on hand, and an old spoon or clean paintbrush for mixing. If the coloring medium you plan to add is toxic, also make sure you use utensils and containers that you'll never use for preparing or serving food!

To prepare the paper and apply the paste, you'll need a water-filled sink or shallow tray; some sponges or a squeegee; and a few high-quality, wide paintbrushes. (Although it isn't required, a rubber brayer can be helpful for spreading the paste.) A smooth, waterproof work surface—one that's easy to clean when you're finished—is a must. A sheet of glass or acrylic, a laminated board, a table covered with a plastic tablecloth, or a table with an enamel top are ideal. If you're not working in your kitchen, fill a bucket of water for cleaning your patterning tools and paintbrushes. Making paste paper is downright messy. For some people, that's exactly what makes this craft so much fun! If you're the tidy type, however, you might want to wear a pair of latex or rubber gloves and an apron.

To dry the finished paste paper, place it on a sweater-drying rack, a clean window screen, or newspapers. Paste-paper sheets should always be dried flat; never hang them up vertically.

Making Paste Paper

One of the most appealing aspects of making paste paper is that no two sheets are ever quite alike. Why? Because the paste recipe you use; the colors, paper, and tools you choose; and the motions you make as you pull or press your designs will result in magical combinations that no one else—including you—will ever be able to replicate. As a form of creative expression, very few decorative techniques can compare with the art of paste paper.

MAKING THE PASTE

Paste recipes abound. Most call for mixing water with wheat starch, cornstarch, or a mixture of flours. Start with one of the paste recipes that follow and see how you like it. For a smooth look, go with the cornstarch recipe; for more texture, choose the stiffer, granular flour paste. For a very smooth, translucent paste, try the wheat starch recipe.

It's a good idea to make the paste several hours or even the day before you begin your project, to help it thicken properly. Just remove any skin that forms on the surface before using the paste.

Mixed-Flours Paste

3/4 cup rice flour

3/4 cup pastry flour

4 3/4 cups cold water

1/2 teaspoon castile soap or glycerin

Pour 3 cups of the cold water into a saucepan and set the pan on the stove over high heat. While you're waiting for it to come to a boil, combine the rice and pastry flours in a mixing bowl. Slowly add the remaining cold water to the flour, stirring constantly, until no lumps remain. Then gradually stir the flour mixture into the boiling water. Add the soap or glycerin (either will help the paste stay supple), and continue to stir over heat until the paste has thickened. Transfer the paste to a resealable container.

Tips

- Essential oils—including clove, cedar, and peppermint—are available at many health-food stores, and glycerin can be purchased at pharmacies.
- For a thinner paste, add more water as you make it. If the paste is too thin, cook it longer, but be sure to stir it constantly. Thinner pastes yield smoother surfaces; thicker pastes provide more texture to designs.
- If you don't plan to use your paste within two or three days, place it in the refrigerator.

Cornstarch Paste

1 cup cornstarch

7 cups cold water

1 teaspoon liquid dish soap

1 teaspoon glycerin

½ teaspoon oil of clove, cedar, or peppermint

Mix the cornstarch with 1 cup of cool water in a large bowl. Pour the rest of the water into a saucepan and bring it to a boil. Then quickly add the hot water to the cornstarch (don't delay), blending the ingredients constantly with an electric mixer. Stir in the liquid soap, glycerin, and one of the oils. (The oils are natural pesticides and will deter silverfish and other bugs from attacking the starch in your projects. Some people also find that oil of clove helps to preserve the paste's color.) Cover the bowl with plastic wrap and leave the paste at room temperature overnight. The next day, remove and discard any skin that has formed and, if necessary, mix the paste in a blender to remove any lumps. The paste should have the consistency of honey. Pour it into a resealable container.

Wheat (or Rice) Starch Paste

¼ cup wheat or rice starch

1¾ cups cold water

2 drops oil of clove

Wheat starch is available from book-art suppliers. Rice starch, which can be found at many oriental food stores, will produce a paste that's not quite as translucent, but which will be perfectly adequate.

Place some ice cubes in a large mixing bowl and set the bowl in the freezer. Pour 1½ cups of the water into a small saucepan and set the pan over high heat to bring it to a boil. Fill the lower portion of a double boiler with water and bring this to a boil as well.

As the two pans are heating, whisk together the starch and the remaining ¼ cup of cold water in the upper portion of the double boiler to create a milky slurry. Place this pan over the lower portion of the double boiler, add the boiling 1½ cups of water to the slurry (it will turn translucent almost immediately), and stir constantly for 5 minutes over heat.

1 Adding color to the paste

Remove the mixing bowl from the freezer, add cold water, and float the hot pan of paste in the water. Add the oil of clove to the paste and, in order to prevent lumps from forming, stir the paste constantly as it cools.

COLORING AND APPLYING THE PASTE

For each color you want to mix, pour ¾ to 1 cup of paste into a container and stir in 1 to 2 teaspoons of color, adding more as desired (Photo 1). When it comes to how much color to add, personal preference rules. (Inexpensive paints have less pigment in them, so you may have to add more of them to achieve the color you desire.) Paste colors usually look lighter after they've dried. If you're new to making paste paper, it's a good idea to test the color of your paste by applying some to a small sheet of scrap paper. Coat the sheet with paste (see page 26) and allow the paste to dry thoroughly. If the finished color is too light, just add more color to the container of paste.

Before you apply the paste to your project paper, you may want to read pages 27-29; they offer a brief introduction to the many different methods for creating beautiful paste-paper designs. You'll need to work fast once the paste is on the paper because it dries so quickly, but don't fret about mistakes. If you goof or don't like a design, just add more paste or rebrush the surface and start again.

To keep the paste from drying too quickly, and to give you more time to work, always apply the paste to damp paper. First, moisten a sheet of paper by dipping it into a water-filled sink or shallow tray. Then hold the paper up for

2 Letting the excess water drip away

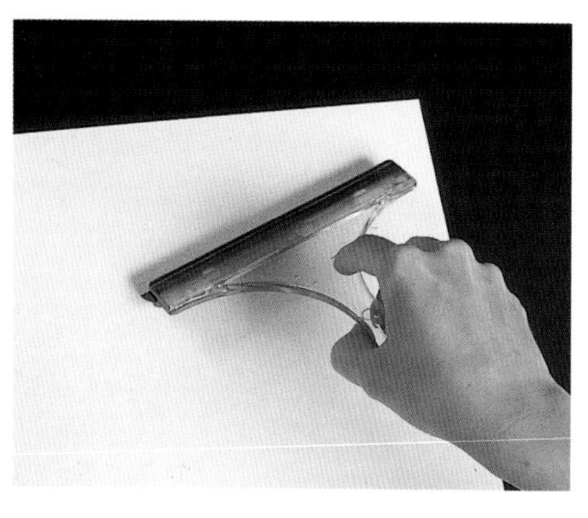

3 Wiping the paper with a squeegee

4 Applying multiple colors to the paper

a few seconds, tilting it slightly to let the excess water drip from one corner at the bottom (Photo 2).

Next, place the paper on your work surface. Starting at one end of the paper and working toward the other, wipe the paper with a sponge or squeegee to smooth it down. (Photo 3). Your goals are to glue the paper to the work surface with water and to remove all air bubbles; any bubbles that remain will show when you smooth on the paste and will disrupt your design.

To cover the sheet with a single color, place a dollop of paste in the center of the paper. Using a wide paintbrush, spread the dollop to cover the paper with a thin layer of paste. (You may also start by applying a thick strip of paste to one end of the paper and brushing it across the sheet.) Be careful not to slather on too much paste, or the overloaded paper may rip as you work. (As they dry, papers to which you've applied too much paste in some areas may crack and peel, or they may buckle, and you won't be able to flatten them out again.) To cover the entire sheet evenly, brush it first in one direction, then in the opposite direction. You may want to smooth the surface further by rolling a rubber brayer across it.

If you're a beginner, it's easiest to apply only one color to the paper and then create your design on it. It's possible to apply multiple colors, however, by brushing on adjacent strips of paste (Photo 4). Use different brushes for each color you apply to avoid mixing the colors. You may also

Tips

- If you plan to create more than one paste-paper sheet, clean your work surface after pasting each one. If you don't, two problems will arise: You'll end up mixing the old colors with the new, and leftover paste on the work surface will glue the new sheet to any drying surface on which you place it.
- Dried paste can be difficult to remove, so as soon as you've finished using a tool or brush, clean it right away, before the paste dries on it.
- To keep the paste-paper design crisp and clear, when you're using a tool to imprint or pull a design in the paste, wipe the tool off occasionally.

want to experiment by adding one color of paste on top of another, but remember that if you use two complementary colors such as red and green, they may blend and cause the colors to become muddy.

DRYING THE PASTE PAPER

When you've finished decorating your paste paper, spread the sheet flat (paste side up) on a sweater-drying rack, a screen, or newspapers. After the paper has dried completely, flatten it by pressing it for a few days between two pieces of smooth fiberboard with heavy weights on top, or just place weights such as books right on top of the paper. Ironing the dried paper on the wrong side will also flatten it.

Creating Designs

Paste paper is an amazingly versatile material, in part because it's so flexible. You'll find a number of paste-paper projects in this book, but don't hesitate to use this material in other ways, too; paste paper makes an ideal gift wrap and lovely stationery (Photo 5).

5

Paste-paper gift wrap and stationery

The most visually captivating designs are sometimes those that exhibit tension through the contrast in their patterns or colors, straight and wavy lines, blurred and crisp images, or hard and soft imprints. Other beautiful designs make use of complementary papers and paste colors.

For a traditional look, experiment with symmetrical patterns. For a more contemporary appearance, try asymmetrical designs. Colors can evoke different eras, too: Muted shades tend to look more old-fashioned; bright hues seem modern. Many paste papers feature allover repeat patterns.

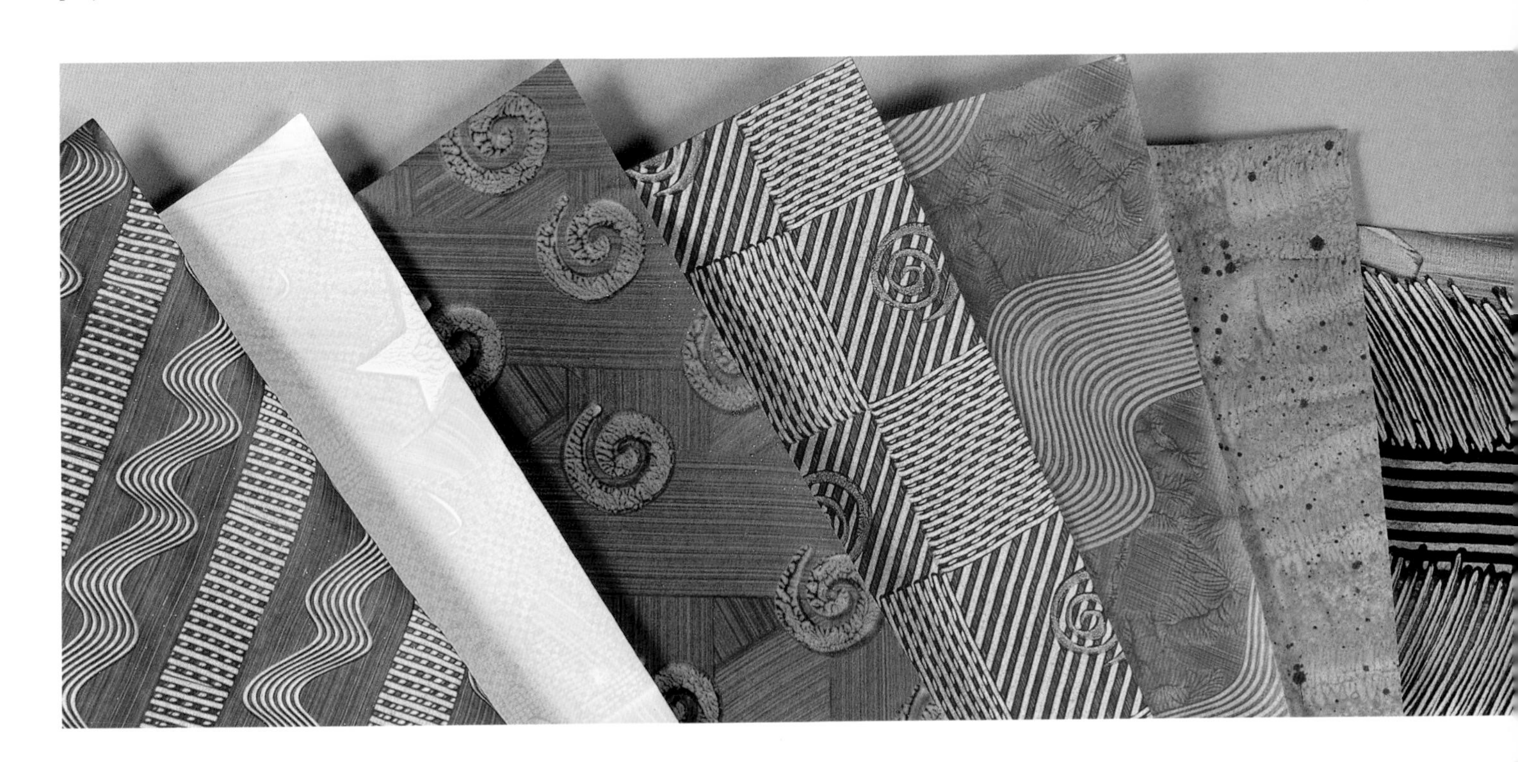

6 Combing the first pass on paper

7 Handiwork

8 Stamped paste-paper designs

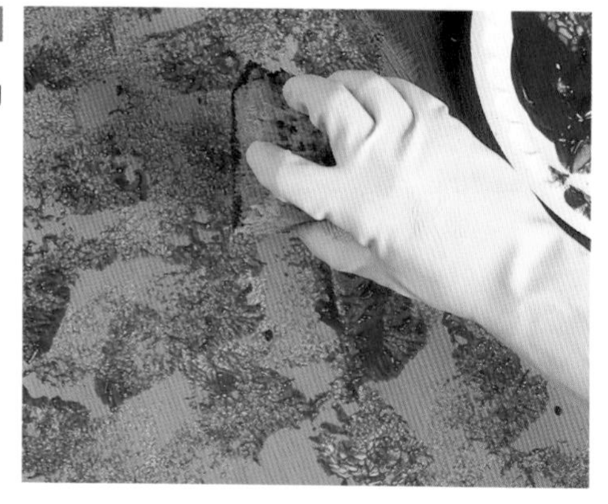

9 Sponging

Explore the many motifs that are possible, including criss-cross lines, circles, or lines of varying widths. Use the following techniques alone or in combination. As you'll see in the projects in this book, artists combine paste-paper techniques with other paper crafts and art forms to create stunning designs.

BRUSHING AND STIPPLING

Brushes of various widths and bristle types can make interesting designs on paste paper. Try swiping a dry brush randomly over pasted paper for a feathered effect. Dab the ends of the brush bristles onto the paper repeatedly to stipple it.

COMBING

Make grooves in the paste by running a wood-graining comb (which has flat teeth), a calligraphy pen (for fine detailing), or similar object through it (Photo 6). You'll unveil the paper's underlying color as you gently scrape away the paste. Tilt the tool toward you to help it glide more smoothly; then pull it in a straight line, in a curved pattern, or in zigzags. Be firm, but take care not to tear the wet paper.

HANDIWORK

This is where those childhood finger-painting skills come in. Run a fingertip through the paste in a circular, swirling motion to create curls, for example. Or press the paper with base of your palm to form random patterns (Photo 7).

STAMPING

Use rubber stamps, carved erasers, bottle caps, and other objects to press repeated patterns or single images into the paste (Photo 8). For repeats, try a brayer with designs cut into it.

SPONGING

Remember making sponge paintings in school? Well, you can press sponges into paste, too (Photo 9). The different shapes and sizes of the sponge's holes will give the paper a textured look. To achieve other textured effects, press crumpled waxed paper, plastic wrap, or aluminum foil into the paste or pull these materials across the paste. The images created make good backgrounds for additional designs.

PULLED PAPER

During the sixteenth through eighteenth centuries, artisans created book covers and endpapers using this technique and its variations. Spread paste over two sheets of paper; then press the sheets together. Or spread the paste over a single sheet and fold the paper over onto itself. Then pull the sheets (or sheet) apart to see veined, almost terrainlike images on each sheet (Photo 10). For a colorful variation, press together sheets that you've pasted with different colors and then pull them apart. The colors will mix here and there in a free-form fashion. For another variation on this technique, place some string, lace, felt strips, or leaves between the sheets before pressing them. Then pull the papers apart and remove the objects, which will have picked up the paste. Their outlines will remain.

PAPER IMPRESSIONS

Place a piece of paper on top of a sheet that has been pasted. Draw a design on the back of the top sheet using a burnisher or similar tool, or press on the back hard with your fingertips. Then quickly lift up the top sheet. The bottom sheet will have a blotted, textured pattern on it.

DOUBLE PASTING

Take a piece of paper that you've already pasted, decorated, and dried. Dampen the paper again and coat it with more paste—perhaps paste of a different color or paste that you've jazzed up with metallic paints. Then create new patterns and designs to create a double image (Photo 11).

MULTICOLORED BACKGROUNDS

Paint a dry sheet of paper with acrylics—no paste, just paint—with any design you like, in any color or colors. After the paint has dried, coat the paper with paste of a different color or colors. As you displace the paste with patterns, the contrasting colors underneath will shine through. Alternatively, instead of starting by painting paper, just apply the paste to sturdy, printed gift wrap or other printed paper (Photo 12).

10 Pulling the papers apart

11 Combing a new design on double-pasted paper

12 Combing through paste applied to printed gift wrap

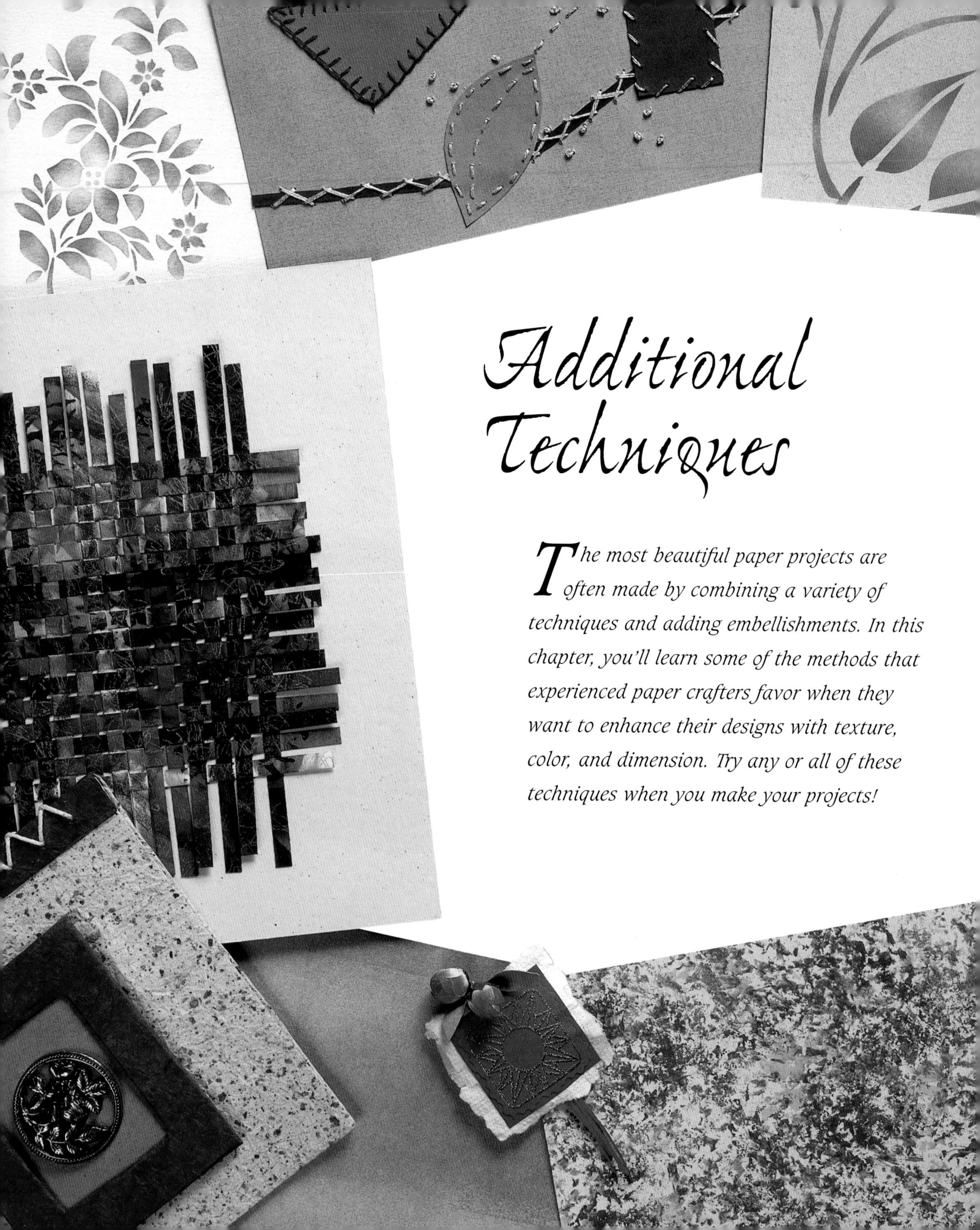

Additional Techniques

The most beautiful paper projects are often made by combining a variety of techniques and adding embellishments. In this chapter, you'll learn some of the methods that experienced paper crafters favor when they want to enhance their designs with texture, color, and dimension. Try any or all of these techniques when you make your projects!

Manipulating Paper

Paper crafters often start by taking advantage of the many ways to manipulate the paper itself. Folding, tearing, cutting, feathering, crimping, layering, and weaving paper are all common techniques.

CREATING DECORATIVE EDGES

For a bold look, tear your paper instead of cutting it. For an even, fairly straight edge, tear along its grain (in the direction that the paper fibers run); tear against the grain for a ragged effect. To determine the direction of the grain, bend the paper slightly. If it bends easily, you're bending in the direction of the grain. If it resists, you're bending against the grain.

Feathering the edges of paper lends a soft appearance to projects. This technique works best with papers with loosely woven fibers, such as mulberry paper, oriental decorative papers, and handmade papers. Dampen the paper edges with water; then gently pull the paper's fibers apart with your fingers.

For more formal decorative edges, choose from the wide variety of decorative-edge scissors that are available. These will cut scallops, deckle edges, zipper patterns, and many other designs as well.

1

Plain weaving with strips of paste paper

CRIMPING

Crimped paper, the surface of which looks similar to corrugated cardboard, adds texture and shadows to projects. Paper-crimping tools, with rollers through which the paper is run, are available commercially and are very easy to use.

WEAVING

To create a basic plain-weave structure with paper, start by cutting a batch of paper strips. If you're a beginner, you may want to start out with strips of equal widths, although many wonderful and very creative weavings are made with strips of different widths and different shapes, such as curves and scallops. If you like, you may cut your strips from sheets of paper that are different colors. Arrange one set of strips vertically, leaving slight gaps between them. To help hold the strips together as you start weaving, secure one edge of the arrangement with clamps or artist's tape. (You may remove these after you've woven several strips and reapply them whenever necessary.)

To begin weaving, thread a strip horizontally through the vertical strips, taking it under the first strip, over the next, under the next, and so on. Weave the next horizontal strip over, under, over, and so on. The plain-weave structure is characterized by its alternating under-over and over-under pattern (Photo 1). To finish off, fold all the loose ends to the back and glue them down.

2

Weaving in three dimensions

3

Layering paper

To customize this basic plain weave, use strips of various widths; cover two or more vertical strips with a horizontal strip to create an irregular weave; weave with curved or zigzag strips; weave twisted strands of paper; or mix plain, patterned, or colored papers.

To weave a three-dimensional piece such as the tote bag shown on page 46, start by weaving the flat bottom portion. Then place a cardboard template diagonally over the weaving and bend the ends of the strips upward around its edges. You'll find that the vertical strips are now slanted diagonally (Photo 2) and that the strips extending from any given side of the square cross the strips from the adjacent side of the square.

To weave the vertical walls, start at any corner of the square and weave together the strips that cross one another. When a strip is too short to weave, lengthen it by gluing a strip of the same color to it, overlapping the ends of the two strips and concealing the joint within the weaving structure. Straighten and tighten all the weavers before attaching new lengths and try to stagger the joints so they don't all occur in the same area of the design. Instructions for finishing off the upper rim are provided on pages 47–48.

LAYERING PAPER

Collage is the art of gluing layers of paper (and sometimes other elements) together to form a design (Photo 3). The process can be as simple as stacking papers of contrasting textures or colors (perhaps with feathered or torn edges) on top of each other in an artful fashion, or as intricate as arranging hundreds of paper cutouts to make a tableau.

Collage artists use various products to glue the cutouts in place. A glue stick or glue pen works for lightweight papers. Craft glue is fine for medium-weight or heavyweight papers, but lightweight papers will soak up the glue's moisture and buckle. A thin, water-based glue is one popular medium for collage, and acrylic matte medium is another.

Tips

- When folding paper, measure the paper first and use a pencil to mark it lightly at the top and bottom edges of the fold line. Next, use a stylus or the edge of a bone folder to score (press a groove into) the paper along the fold line. Then fold the paper over a straightedge placed at the score line (the score should be on the outside of the fold), and crease the fold with a bone folder or a similar burnishing tool.
- The accordion fold is an attractive variation that's sometimes used to make journal pages. Measure and mark your paper for several folds of equal width; then fold the paper back and forth on top of itself until you've pleated the entire sheet.

Surface Treatments

If you're just starting out with paper crafts, you may be surprised to discover the many choices available for adding texture and color to ordinary paper. From simple sponging and spattering to applying beautiful stenciled accents, an almost limitless world of paper decoration awaits you. Start by taking a trip to your local art-supply or craft store and stocking up on your favorite coloring media.

- **Colored pencils** work well on all but glossy coated papers. Blend them to create new colors, or vary the intensity of their individual colors by applying more or less pressure on them as you draw. These pencils are great for outlining the edges of layered papers, for filling in stamped outlines and—when they're rubbed on gently—for coloring the raised ridges of dry-embossed surfaces.

- **Pastels and chalks** are best suited for porous, bond papers. Soften the edges of colored areas or blend different colors by rubbing them gently with a cotton ball, wad of tissue, or fingertip. Spray the colors with a fixative to help prevent smearing.

- **Pens and markers** make it easy to draw a flourish here and there, and they come in many forms. Fine-pointed and wide-tipped, permanent and water-based, and metallic and embossing versions are all available.

- **Paints** remain a favorite way to embellish paper with color. Puff paints also lend wonderful textures to paper. When they're heated with an embossing gun, they become three-dimensional. Watercolors, which come in cakes, in tubes, and in pencil and pen form, are perfect for creating delicately washed backgrounds. Watercolor pencils and markers are especially good for adding color accents to permanent, waterproof stamped images. Acrylic paints are also versatile and feature such specialty paints as metallics, opalescents, fluorescents and glitters, in addition to solid colors.

- **Powdered pearlescent pigments** are a great way to add luminescence to your projects. Dust a little over embossing powder to add iridescence to a stamped or stenciled image that you're about to emboss with a heat gun. Or brush or sponge some pigment onto your paper as an accent; then seal it with an acrylic spray. You can also mix powdered pigments with glue, gum arabic, acrylics, or other viscous substances and apply them as if they were paints.

- **Glitter** spices up projects with sparkling colors. Mix ultrafine glitter into colored paste; your finished paste paper will twinkle. Sprinkle glitter over embossed, stenciled, or stamped images to add texture and shininess, or accent your works with dabs from glitter glue pens.

STENCILING

Stenciling is a wonderful way to decorate paper with color and images. You'll need a palette, an applicator, a colored medium, stencils, and paper. Waxed paper or a foam plate will make a great palette. For color application, stencilers usually use stencil brushes, but many use foam brushes,

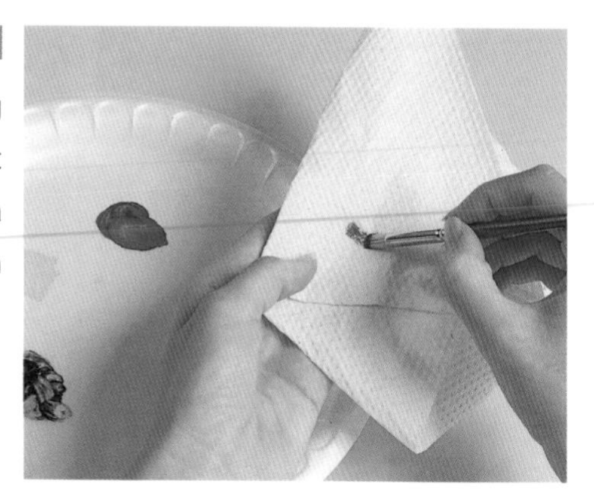

4 Removing excess paint from a stencil brush

5 Coloring with a stencil brush—and a light touch

foam brayers, sponges, and cloths as well. Almost any paper can be stenciled, including watercolor paper, drawing paper, and even handmade paper.

Beginners should start with creamy stenciling paints. These condensed oils (sold at craft stores in pots and as sticks or crayons) are less likely than other coloring media to seep under the stencil and cause blurring. Regular acrylics and those designed especially for stenciling are commonly used as well; some artists add a commercial stencil medium to them. The pigment, dye, fabric, and embossing inks that stampers favor also work for stenciling and may be applied with stencil brushes, sponges, or foam brayers.

Ready-made plastic and brass stencils are widely available, but many stencilers use found objects or carve their own stencils from acetate with a craft knife.

Start by taping your stencil to the paper with removable tape. If you're coloring with an oil stick, remove the skin that forms on the stick's surface and then smear the paint onto your palette. Tap your stencil brush into the smeared paint to load the bristles. If you're using an oil creme pot, dip the brush directly into the jar. To use acrylic paint, put it onto the palette and dip the brush into the pool of paint.

Next, swirl the brush on a paper towel or scrap paper until it is dry to the touch (Photo 4). This will remove excess paint and will help to distribute the paint evenly through the bristles. Whether you use a stencil brush or another applicator, don't leave much medium on your applicator, or it may bleed under the stencil's edges.

Now color in the stencil with your "dry" brush, starting at the edges of the stencil outline and brushing inward toward the center of the design. You may stipple with the brush by holding it upright and tapping its bristles onto the paper, or swirl (rouge) the brush in circular strokes. Work from the lightest hue to the darkest, using a different brush for each color. If you like, blend colors to form new ones. Build the color gradually, to avoid bleeding or seepage, and use a light touch (Photo 5). As you gain more experience, try applying different levels of pressure to produce darker or lighter shades of color in sections of the design.

When you're finished, remove the tape, lift the stencil straight up to avoid smudges, and allow the colored image to dry. Before the media dry, clean the stencil and brushes with soap and water or with turpentine or a commercial brush cleaner, depending on the type of media. Hot water and a nylon scouring pad help when you're removing acrylic paints from sturdy stencils.

APPLYING SOLID COLORS

To apply a solid color (one of the best techniques for coloring background papers), coat the entire surface of a rubber brayer with a nonpermanent-ink pad, nonpermanent markers, or watercolor paints. Then roll the brayer over

Tip

- When cutting a stencil from acetate, cut out the small areas before the larger ones so that you won't break the stencil as you carve it. Use hole punches to pierce small decorative shapes.

your paper, repeating and overlapping your strokes until the paper is covered. For a multicolored background, ink the brayer with a rainbow pad or run it over a tray of watercolors that you've squeezed from their tubes. (Wetting the paper first will help paints go on more smoothly.)

CREATING COLORED PATTERNS

To create stripes, hold a nonpermanent-ink marker against the roller and rotate the roller until you've inked its circumference with a colored line. Repeat this process, using as many different colored markers as you wish, until you've drawn several lines around the roller. Then roll the brayer across the paper to create lines. To create a plaid design, just roll a second set of lines, perpendicular to the first. If you don't want straight lines, draw squiggles on the roller. Aching for polka dots? Use the marker to draw dots all over the brayer, and then go to town!

SPONGING

Sponging is a great way to decorate backgrounds and to embellish foregrounds. Dab a foam wedge, household, or sea sponge onto a nonpermanent-ink pad, dip the sponge into paint on a palette, or color it with a marker. Then lightly blot or brush color onto your paper. (Use a different sponge for each color.) For textured backgrounds, crinkle some waxed paper, plastic wrap, or a paper towel. Then ink the scrunched-up wad on a pad or press it into paint spread on a palette, and dab your paper with it.

SPATTERING

Load an old, stiff-bristled toothbrush or a spatter brush with stamping ink or a variety of paints. Then pull back lightly on the bristles with your thumbnail, a blunt knife, or a stiff card to spatter flecks of color across the paper. (Always pull bristles toward you to avoid spattering yourself.) Try spattering over stencils, or spatter colored paste over paste-paper designs. Another variation: Spatter color over and beyond the edges of a solid template (or a flat, natural object such as a leaf) that you have placed on top of your paper. When you lift up the template or object, its outline will remain.

Three-Dimensional Decorations

Buttons, beads, and bows are easy to sew, glue, or string onto your designs and add a wonderful, tactile quality to your works. Almost any project can benefit from a bit of added lace or other fabric snippets. For elegance or whimsy, cascade a few cords, tassels, metallic threads, or ribbons down the surface of a greeting card, or string pretty buttons or beads on it. And don't forget some of nature's finest designs: dried flowers, leaves, and shells.

Paper crafters use a variety of threads and embroidery flosses, both to bind handmade journals and to embellish their designs. Stitches themselves can be artistic elements. Place the paper under the needle of your sewing machine and run random stitches across the surface. Try a few straight or zigzag stitches; these can make a border around a design element. Hand-sewn stitches look great, too.

Setting Up

As a paper crafter, you won't need a high-tech workshop, but you will need a comfortable work area and some basic tools and materials.

Your Work Area

A clean, hard, large work surface is a must. Covering this surface with sheets of newsprint will keep it clean. A few projects require a waterproof surface, such as a laminated countertop or a table covered with a plastic tablecloth. Make sure you have adequate light and ventilation, as well as easy access to soap and water for cleanup. For some techniques, such as paste paper, you'll also need cooking utensils and a heating element, so you may want to set up shop in your kitchen. (If you're working with pastes or other messy substances, waterproof yourself by wearing an apron and latex or rubber gloves!)

Basic Materials and Tools

Avid paper crafters make use of the same basic tools and supplies over and over again. How will you know which of these to purchase? First, read the descriptions that follow.

Then pick the project you want to make and read the step-by-step instructions that come with it; the instructions always make mention of the basic tools and supplies that are required.

- **Adhesives.**
  - White craft glue is suitable for many crafting tasks.
  - Thin, water-based craft glue, which is thinner than the typical white craft glue, is useful for layering papers.
  - Spray mount adhesive is best for gluing very thin papers together or for mounting papers smoothly onto other surfaces.
  - Glue sticks and glue pens are used for gluing lightweight papers, for heat embossing, and for applying glitter.
  - Hot (or cool-melt) glue guns will help you attach beads and other decorative items to paper.
  - Acrylic matte medium is designed for mixing into acrylic paints to alter their characteristics, but it's also great as an adhesive. (Use fluid matte medium to join layers of paper and gel matte medium to hold heavier, three-dimensional objects such as beads.)
  - Rubber cement will glue paper to paper, but it has a tendency to bleed over time.
  - Tapes for papers include cellophane, removable (low-tack), masking, and double-sided.

- **Bone folders.** Available at art-supply stores, these are simply burnishers made for creasing paper and smoothing surfaces.

- **Brayers.** Foam and rubber brayers are used to ink stamps, flatten layers of paper, cover large surfaces quickly with paint or ink, spread paste, and color stencils. A brayer may also be used to print repeat patterns.

- **Coloring accessories.** These vary widely and include colored pencils; pastels and chalks; pens and markers; paints such as acrylics, watercolors, and gouache; powdered pigments; and glitter. (See "Surface Treatments" on page 33.)

- **Craft knives.** These make precise cuts. Swiveling-blade models are best for curved cuts.

- **Commercial self-healing cutting mats.** A mat will protect your work surface, but a piece of glass with well-taped edges, an inverted glass baking dish, a very thick piece of smooth cardboard, or a stack of paper will make an adequate substitute.

- **Paintbrushes.** Keep a variety of foam brushes as well as soft- and stiff-bristled brushes on hand. You'll need watercolor brushes for applying paints and wide brushes for applying glue, paste, or varnish.

- **Palettes.** You'll mix paints or pigments on their surfaces. Plastic or foam plates will also work.

- **Pencils and rulers.** Cork-backed rulers won't slide around, and ink won't seep under them. Transparent rulers with grids help with precise measurements. Mark fold lines and measurements with pencils.

- **Scissors.** Depending on the project you choose, you'll need large paper scissors, fabric scissors, or small scissors for cutting detailed shapes.

- **Scrap paper and sticky notes.** You'll use either scrap paper or sticky notes for masking stamps and scrap paper for testing your designs.

- **Sewing needles.** Use these when a project calls for beading, stitching, or binding.

- **Spatter brushes or old toothbrushes.** For details on spattering, see page 35.

- **Sponges.** Household sponges are used to apply inks and paints, and to create textured patterns (sea sponges also work for this technique).

- **Water containers.** You'll need a spray bottle for moistening paper, a shallow tray for dipping paper, and jars or bowls for rinsing brushes.

Gift Card, Envelope, and Box

Show that your present is from the heart with a card, envelope, and gift box made especially for your friend or loved one. You can almost smell the lavender and feel the brush of fern fronds against your skin as you gaze on these treasures. The key to these projects is the random stamping of fern images on both the front and back of lavender mulberry paper. The stamps on the back appear as quietly elegant shadows through this almost translucent paper.

The Card

1 Using the fern stamp and the green metallic ink, randomly stamp both the back (the slightly rougher surface) and the front of the lavender mulberry paper until the images cover the sheet. Re-ink between stampings as desired; partly inked images can lend a lovely, feathered appearance to the design.

2 Ink an old toothbrush or a spatter brush with the purple stamp pad and spritz the bristles with water from a spray bottle to dilute the ink slightly. Randomly spatter the purple ink over the paper's front surface.

3 Fold the 6" x 8½" eggplant card stock in half to make a 4¼" x 6" card.

4 Using the Victorian-edge scissors, trim the edges of the dark lavender paper so the paper is slightly narrower than the front of the card all the way around.

5 Center the dark lavender paper on the front of the folded card stock and glue it in place.

6 Feather the edges of the 3½" x 5¼" piece of green mulberry paper. Center the feathered paper on the dark lavender paper and glue it in place.

7 To create the card's centerpiece, cut a piece of the stamped lavender paper to fit the 2⅝" x 3½" bristol board. (Cut this from one corner of the stamped sheet, as you'll need the rest to line the envelope and cover the gift box and lid.) Then glue the cutout to the bristol board, front surface up.

8 Glue one end of the silver metallic thread to the back of the bristol-board centerpiece. Then wrap the thread around it vertically four times, as shown in the photo. Cut the thread and glue the end to the back of the board.

9 Cut two or three strands of silver metallic thread and three narrow satin ribbons, each about 13" long. Then knot the threads and ribbons together in the center. Wrap some additional metallic thread around the knot to conceal it.

10 Arrange the ribbons and threads as shown in the project photo, glue the knot to the card, and curl the ribbons slightly.

11 Glue the centerpiece and then the dried lavender or other dried flowers onto the card as desired. Glue the ribbon to the card wherever necessary.

The Envelope

1 Make a photocopy of figure 1 (see page 40), enlarging it to the dimension shown. Cut out the enlarged photocopy, which will serve as a template for the envelope.

MATERIALS AND TOOLS

Stamping tools and supplies (see pages 15–18)

Lavender mulberry paper, about 25" x 36"

Eggplant card stock, 6" x 8½"

Eggplant card stock, 8½" x 11"

Dark lavender paper, 4¼" x 6"

Green mulberry paper, 3½" x 5¼"

Green mulberry paper, 8" x 8"

Green mulberry paper, 5" x 5"

Heavyweight white bristol board, 2⅝" x 3½"

Heavyweight white bristol board, 9" x 9"

Heavyweight white bristol board, 5½" x 5½"

Green metallic pigment-ink stamp pad

Any purple ink stamp pad

Silver metallic thread, one spool

Several narrow satin ribbons in complementary colors, each 1 yard long

Wide silver metallic ribbon, 1 yard long

Dried lavender or other dried flowers

Fern stamp (Rubber Stampede, #A1128E)

Victorian-edge decorative scissors

BASIC TECHNIQUES

Stamping (see pages 14–21)

Creating decorative edges (see page 31)

Layering paper (see page 32)

Spattering (see page 35)

2 Trace the outline of the template onto the 8½" x 11" eggplant card stock and cut along the traced lines.

3 Using figure 1 as a guide, place the cut card stock face down and fold the side flaps in. Then fold the bottom flap up and glue it to the tabs.

4 Cut a 6" x 7¼" piece of the stamped lavender mulberry paper. Slide this paper lining, face up, into the envelope until it touches the bottom and trim it to fit, leaving a ¼"-wide strip of the envelope's top flap exposed at the top. (You'll apply glue to this exposed portion when you're ready to seal the envelope.)

5 Tack the lining to the inside of the envelope with glue.

Figure 1

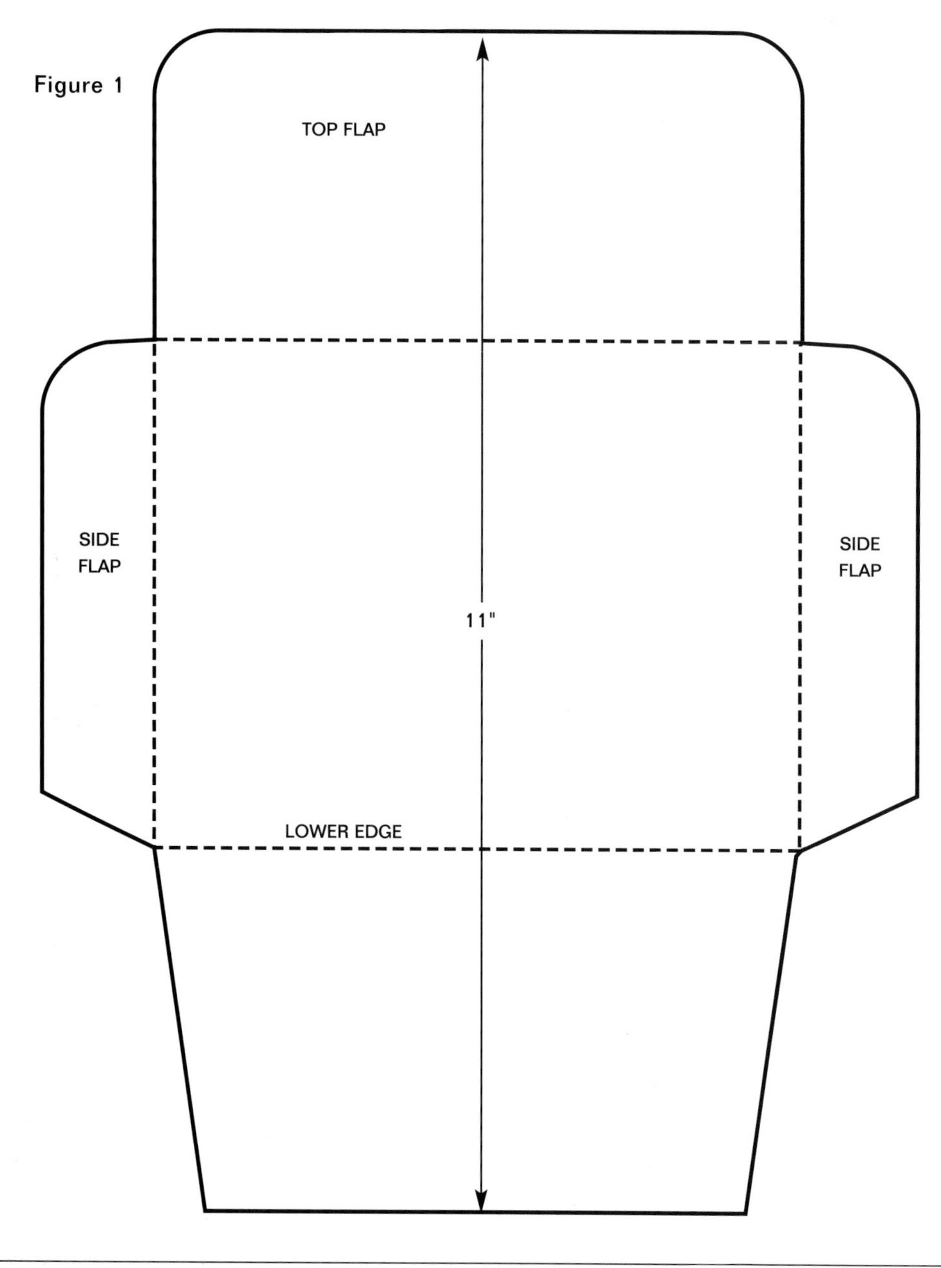

The Box

1 Figure 2, opposite, represents three templates: one for the box lid (black), one for its paper lining (green), and one for its paper covering (lavender). Figure 3, opposite, also represents three templates: the box (black), the paper that will line the interior of the box (green), and the paper that will cover the exterior of the box (lavender). Make three photocopies of each figure, enlarging them to the dimensions shown. Cut a different template from each photocopy and label each one.

2 Trace the box template (fig. 3) onto the 9" x 9" piece of bristol board and cut the board out along the traced lines. Then score and crease

Tips

- When folding the box and lid, be sure to tuck the side flaps underneath the other portions; the flaps should be hidden after assembly.
- For larger or smaller boxes and lids, just make larger or smaller photocopies of the templates (figs. 2 and 3). Do be sure you increase or decrease the lid and box sizes by the same amount, or the assembled box and lid won't fit together.

the board along the dotted fold lines shown on the template.

3 Trace the template for the box's paper covering onto the piece of stamped lavender mulberry paper and cut the paper along the traced lines. Then glue the paper covering onto the outer face of the box.

4 Fold the paper-covered box at the creased lines and glue the tabs in place to hold the box together. Then fold the excess paper covering over the top edges of the box and glue it down.

5 Trace the template for the box's lining onto the 8" x 8" green mulberry paper and cut the paper out. Then glue this paper lining onto the inside of the box.

6 Repeat steps 2 through 5 to cut, cover, and line the lid (fig. 2), using the 5½" x 5½" bristol board for the lid, the stamped lavender mulberry paper for the exterior covering, and the 5" x 5" green mulberry paper for the lining.

7 Cut about 7" of the wide silver metallic ribbon, position it across the box top, and glue the ends to the inside of the lid.

8 Tie a big bow, as shown in the project photo, using the silver ribbon and the remaining satin ribbons. Use the leftover silver ribbon to wrap the bow onto the ribbon on the lid.

Figure 2

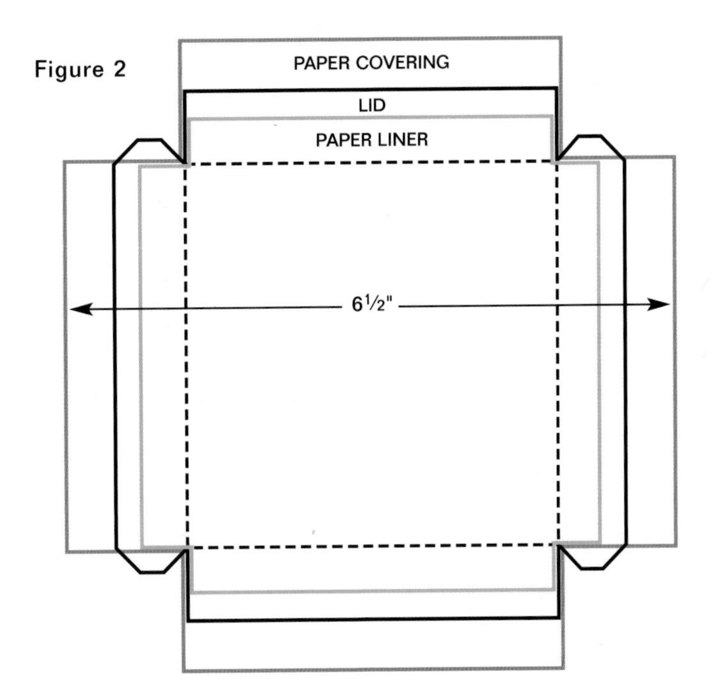

Figure 3

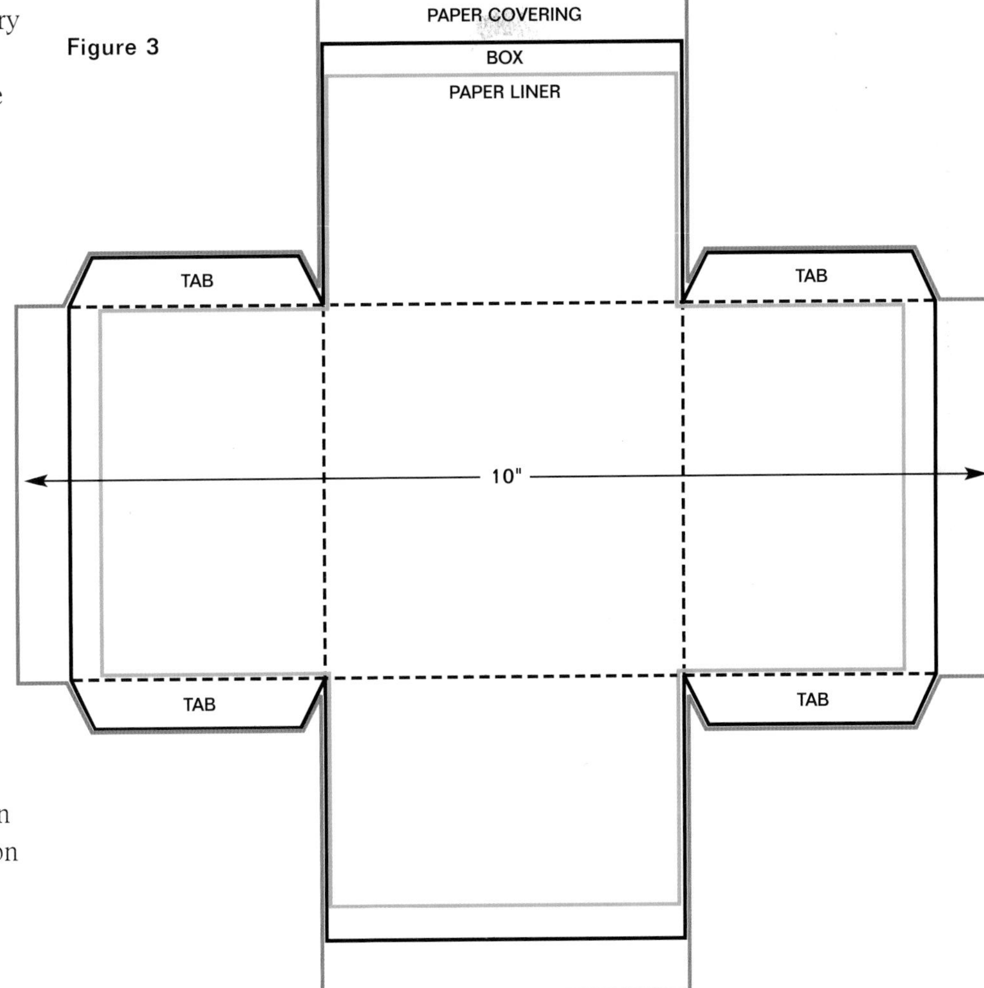

Shadow Box

Imagine traveling to the Orient, packing up a bit of the ambiance while you're there, and taking it home in this beautiful shadow box. The quiet balance of tiles and bamboo, enhanced by decorative papers, reflects the style and sophistication of Asia.

1 Paint the shadow box with the copper acrylic paint and allow it to dry.

2 Using the green pigment ink, stamp the celadon green paper with the bamboo stamp. Glue the paper onto the 5¼" x 7¼" piece of cardboard.

3 Ink the entire surface of the 1¾" x 3½" piece of cardboard with embossing ink by tapping the ink pad directly onto it. Then cover the surface with the bronze embossing powder, tap off any excess powder, and heat emboss the surface.

4 When the embossing powder has cooled, apply a second coat of ink and powder and heat emboss again. Let the surface cool.

5 Ink the bamboo stamp with the green pigment ink and set it aside while you apply a third layer of embossing ink and powder to the cardboard. Heat the powder; when it has melted and while it's still fluid, stamp the surface once with the inked bamboo stamp. (The ink will act as a resist and will prevent the stamp from sticking.) Remove the stamp and let the cardboard tile cool.

6 Repeat steps 3 and 4 with the 2" cardboard square, but this time use the green pigment ink and the clear embossing powder. Let the layers cool.

7 Ink the dragonfly stamp with the black pigment ink and set it aside while you apply a third layer of green ink and powder to the cardboard. Sprinkle a little green and gold powdered pigment onto the tile while heating the third layer of embossing powder. Again, when the powders have melted and are still fluid, stamp the surface. Remove the dragonfly stamp and let the cardboard tile cool.

8 Tear out a small piece of the cream paper that is slightly larger than the dragonfly cardboard tile. Ink the Far East News stamp with the black pigment ink and stamp the paper.

9 Tear out a piece of the mauve paper, making it just large enough to fill with the bamboo stamp. Stamp the paper using the green pigment ink.

10 Paint the bamboo skewer with the black acrylic paint and let it dry; then wrap it with the gold-colored wire, as shown in the project photo.

11 Tear out a piece of the black paper, making it slightly larger than the bamboo cardboard tile.

12 Arrange all the design elements on the cardboard-backed green paper and glue them in place. Insert the green panel into the shadow-box frame and fold down the frame's support tabs to secure it.

BASIC TECHNIQUES

Heat embossing (see pages 11–13)

Stamping (see pages 14–21)

Layering paper (see page 32)

Three-dimensional decorations (see page 35)

MATERIALS AND TOOLS

Heat-embossing tools and supplies (see pages 11–13)

Stamping tools and supplies (see pages 15–18)

Unfinished wooden shadow box, 6" x 8", with a 5¼" x 7¼" opening in the back

Celadon green art paper, 5¼" x 7¼"

Cardboard, 5¼" x 7¼"

Cardboard, 1¾" x 3½"

Cardboard square, 2" x 2"

Three pieces of art paper: mauve, black with gold flecks, and cream, each 4" x 4"

Copper acrylic paint

Green pigment-ink stamp pad

Black pigment-ink stamp pad

Embossing-ink stamp pad

Ultrathick bronze embossing powder

Ultrathick clear embossing powder

Interference green powdered pearlescent pigment

Gold powdered pearlescent pigment

Bamboo skewer, 2¾" long

Black acrylic paint

Gold-colored wire

Bamboo stamp (Rubber Stampede, #A2219E)

Painted dragonfly stamp (Rubber Stampede, #A2297C)

Far East News stamp (Rubber Stampede, #MP24F)

Stamped Ornaments

Layers of tissue paper give these delightful holiday ornaments their delicate, crinkly look. Try pastels for Easter and primary colors for Christmas—it's up to you!

1 Following the manufacturer's instructions, prepare the moldable stylus tips by heating them on a light bulb and then pressing them against the stamps listed in "Materials and Tools."

2 Ink the stylus tips and stamp the images on several sheets of white tissue paper. (You may want to apply background colors to some of the sheets first. To do this, just dab the ink pads directly on the paper.)

- The designs on these ornaments were created with a special stylus (shop for this at your local craft or rubber-stamp store) that is used with two different kinds of replaceable tips: *blender tips* and tips that can be molded. The blender tips, which come in different shapes, are used for stamping, stenciling, brushing, or blending colors on paper. The moldable tips can be heated with a light bulb and then pressed against textured surfaces—often portions of existing rubber stamps—to create new stamps. (These may be reheated and remolded repeatedly.) If you don't have access to this tool, simply use any rubber stamps you like.

3 Heat-set the inks with a craft heat gun and let the papers cool. (This will prevent the inks from bleeding when you glue them to the polystyrene balls.)

4 While the decorated sheets of papers are cooling, tear enough additional strips of white tissue paper to cover the polystyrene ball with several layers. Glue these plain strips to the ball with wallpaper paste.

5 Glue the decorated papers on top of the plain strips with wallpaper paste and let the paste dry.

6 To make a hanger for each ornament, first thread a strand of the gold metallic thread through a sequin and knot its ends together. Then glue the sequin to the ornament with a hot glue gun, hiding the knot under the sequin.

7 Suspend each ornament by its hanger, brush a coat of varnish onto it, and let the varnish dry.

MATERIALS AND TOOLS

Stamping tools and supplies (see pages 15–18)

Several sheets of white tissue paper

Rigid polystyrene balls: seven, each 3" in diameter

ColorToolBox Stylus Tray (Clearsnap, #69004)

Leaves and swirled floral stamp (Magenta, #20.016.P)

Star stamp (Magenta, #28.009.G)

Abstract stamp (Magenta, #23.029.D)

Flower stamp (Magenta, #N-0101)

Floral motif stamp (Magenta, #14.107.F)

Marbled stamp (Magenta, #N-0260)

Floral stamp (Magenta, #14.007.E)

Abstract floral stamp (Magenta, #H-0269)

Permanent fabric or fabric pigment-ink stamp pads, in any colors (raised or removable; see "Tip," page 91)

Wallpaper paste

Varnish

Seven gold sequins

Gold metallic threads: seven, each 12" long

BASIC TECHNIQUES

Stamping (see pages 14–21)

Layering paper (see page 32)

Three-dimensional decorations (see page 35)

Woven Tote Bag

Weave a satchel that's perfect for carrying a canister of mineral water to a picnic. Or wrap up a bottle of fine wine to give to a party hostess; she'll appreciate the thoughtful present, and she can use the sturdy tote again and again. This tote is created using the basic "over-one, under-one" plain weave; you'll find that it's surprisingly easy to make.

1 Prepare two sheets of paste paper, using the heavyweight watercolor paper and your favorite paste recipe (the paste used in this project was made with a mixed-flours recipe). Color one container of paste pink and another purple. Apply one color to each sheet and use a graining comb to create stripes on the two sheets, combing in the same direction as the grain of the paper. Let the sheets of paper dry.

2 Cut the two sheets of paste paper into ½" x 24" strips, making sure that the colored stripes run the length of each strip. Then refer to the plain-weave instructions on page 31.

3 Weave the flat bottom portion of the tote, using ten pink horizontal strips and ten vertical purple strips. Your goal here is to weave a square section in the center of the strips, leaving the ends of the strips free at every edge. (If you stagger the ends of the strips so that their ends aren't all evenly aligned, you'll find that it's much easier to disguise the areas where you'll glue new strips onto the ends of old ones.)

4 Position the 4" x 4" cardboard template diagonally on top of the flat weaving. (Make sure that each corner rests between strips—not on top of a strip.) Bend the woven strips up around the cardboard and begin weaving the walls of the tote on a diagonal (see page 32). Tighten the weave structure periodically as you work. When a strip is too short to weave, lengthen it by gluing a strip of the same color to it, overlapping the ends of the two strips by ½" and concealing the joint within the weaving structure.

5 When the basket is the desired height all the way around, tighten and straighten the weave structure and secure all of the ends with clothespins.

6 To form the decorative serrated rim of the tote, first look at the outer top of the tote and find a straight line of "over-ones" (weavers that cross other strips). The weavers they cross (the "under-ones") will be their mates. Remove the clothespin from an over-one; then bend the strip diagonally down across its mate, toward the inside bottom of the tote. Then bend

MATERIALS AND TOOLS

Paste-paper tools, supplies, and recipes (see pages 23–25 and step 1)

140-pound (or heavier) watercolor paper: two sheets, each 18" x 24"

Pink and purple acrylic paints

Several large bag clamps, about 5" or 6" wide, or removable tape

Cardboard or other stiff paper, 4" x 4"

Clothespins

Binder's board or heavyweight mat board, 4⅛" x 4⅛"

Two ⅛"-diameter cords, each 18" long

Pale pink decorative cord, 2 yards long

BASIC TECHNIQUES

Paste paper (see pages 22–29)

Weaving (see pages 31–32)

the under-one down over the over-one, toward the bottom interior of the tote. Repeat this process all the way around the top of the tote.

7 As you fold the pairs of strips into the interior of the tote, begin using them to weave an inner collar, following the same basic over-one, under-one pattern and working downward into the basket. The collar should be 2" to 3" deep. When you're finished, hold everything in place with clothespins.

8 Using a sharp craft knife, slice a large X-shape from corner to corner of the binder's board. Don't cut the board all the way through (you'll use it to reinforce the bottom of the tote); just cut grooves in it.

9 Coat the grooves with glue and press an 18" length of ⅛" diameter cord into each one until the cords are flush with the surface of the binder's board. (Leave an equal length of cord extending from each corner.) Glue the cords in place.

10 Using leftover paste-paper strips, weave a square large enough to cover one surface of the binder's board. Glue the woven square to the board, covering the grooves and sunken cords. Wrap the edges of the weavers over to the back of the board and glue them in place.

11 If necessary, line the back of the binder's board with paper so that its surface is level. Then glue the board, back side up, to the bottom of the tote, so that its woven surface becomes the tote's new bottom.

12 Place a liquid-filled bottle or a brick inside the tote to weight it down overnight.

13 Thread the four loose cord ends through the corners of the tote bottom, from the outside to the inside. Knot the two ends of each cord together to form two loops inside the tote. Each loop, when held taut, should extend about 6" to 9" up inside the basket. (If the cords show on the outside of the tote, paint them an appropriate shade of pink or purple to mask them.)

14 Pull up on the looped cords inside the tote. Then draw an imaginary line from the upper tip of each looped cord to the serrated rim point above it. (These two serrated points should be directly opposite each other.) Run one end of the thick, decorative cord down through the weaving on one side of one serrated point, through the collar, and into the tote. Loop the cord through the tied cord inside the basket, back up through the collar, and out the other side of the point on top of the tote. Repeat to thread the other end of the cord through the other side of the tote. Adjust the cord ends so that two, even lengths hang over the sides of the tote.

15 Knot the loose ends of the decorative cord. You may use any knot you like, as long as it won't pull apart when you lift the filled tote by grasping the cord.

16 Cut two paper triangles, each 3" long and with a ½" base, from scrap weavers. Roll and glue them around the ends of the cords to cover them.

17 Glue the collar weavers—except those that cover the emerging cord—to the inside of the tote and clamp them down with clothespins until they are dry. (Leaving the weavers that cover the cord ends free will ensure that the weight of the tote is supported by the cord rather than by the paper.)

Tip

- To make a tote with a larger diameter than the one shown in the project photo, just enlarge the size of the flat woven section and of the cardboard template used in step 4.

Book Cover and Bookmark

You can almost picture a young girl of the nineteenth century as she pauses to insert the tasseled bookmark in a book that she has protected with this quaint, paste-paper cover. Delicate beads and gentle embossings help to evoke these thoughts of quiet contemplation in the Victorian era.

MATERIALS AND TOOLS

- Paste-paper tools, supplies, and recipes (see pages 23–25 and step 1)
- Dry-embossing tools and supplies (see pages 7–9)
- White watercolor paper, two sheets, each 18" x 24"
- Brown acrylic paint
- Rubber wedge tool
- Wooden stick or unsharpened pencil
- Aqua card stock, 8" x 12"
- Dark purple card stock, 8" x 12"
- Taupe card stock, 8" x 10"
- 16 amethyst-color niblet-cut (or similar) beads
- 24 aqua/green glass (or similar) beads, size 10
- Aqua embroidery floss
- Amethyst metallic thread
- Victorian corner stencil (American Traditional Stencils, #MS-9)
- Paper crimper

BASIC TECHNIQUES

- Dry embossing (see pages 7–9)
- Paste paper (see pages 22–29)
- Creating decorative edges (see page 31)
- Crimping (see page 31)
- Three-dimensional decorations (see page 35)

The Cover

1 Prepare your paste, coloring it with brown acrylic paint. (The paper for these projects was made with a mixed-flours paste.) Then spread the paste over one sheet of the white watercolor paper and pull a rubber wedge tool through it to form the softly combed patterns. To draw the vertical lines, pull a wooden stick or an unsharpened pencil through the paste. Let the paper dry and flatten it if necessary.

2 To begin making the cover, first measure the width of your book's front cover, the width of its spine, and the width of its back cover. Add these dimensions; then add 5" to 6" to the total. (The added inches will allow you to create front and back flaps that will fold inside the cover.) Measure the book's height and add 2" to allow for finished edges at the top and bottom. On the back of your paste paper, mark a rectangle of these dimensions; then cut the rectangle out.

3 Place the paste paper on a flat surface, face down. Open your book and center it on the paper. Then fold over 1" of the paper at the top of the book and 1" at the bottom to form finished edges. With the book still centered on the paper, fold and crease the paper along both edges of the spine. Then fold and crease the front and back flaps over the book's front and back jackets. Remove the paper from the book.

4 To begin making the cover's central design motif, first cut a 2" square of aqua card stock and a 2½" x 2½" square of purple card stock. Using the Victorian corner stencil and the project photo as a guide, dry emboss the aqua square. Then glue it to the purple square.

5 Using the same stencil, dry emboss a corner motif on a piece of aqua card stock and trim around the motif to form a 1¾" x 1¾" x 2" triangle. Repeat to dry emboss another aqua triangle.

6 Cut two 2¼" x 2¼" x 3¼" triangles from purple card stock. Glue a small, embossed aqua triangle (see step 5) in the center of each one.

7 To arrange the three-piece center motif, first refer to the project photo. Then cut off the purple tip of each layered triangle and arrange the triangles with their trimmed tips on top of two of the layered square's opposing corners. Glue each triangle to the layered square, making sure that the points of the aqua triangles meet the corners of the aqua square.

8 Cut out four pieces of purple card stock and two pieces of aqua card stock, each 2½" square. Create six prairie points with these squares (see "Tip," opposite).

9 Tear out a 4" x 6" rectangle of white watercolor paper. Turn the paper face down and position it as a vertical rectangle. Using the project photo as a guide, center the aqua prairie points along the top and bottom edges of the rectangle and glue them in place. Glue the four purple points in place as well; they should overlap the aqua points. Turn the watercolor paper over. If any purple card stock shows at the edges, trim it away.

10 Measure the length of the assembled triangle-and-square motif. Then crimp the taupe card stock and cut a rectangle from it that is 3¼" wide and the same length as the triangle-and-square motif.

11 Cut two lengths of amethyst metallic thread. String two amethyst beads and three aqua/green beads (refer to the project photo for bead placement) on one thread, knotting the thread to keep the beads from sliding. Repeat this step to create another five-bead set on the same thread and two more sets on the other thread.

12 Arrange the two threads on the front of the crimped card stock and glue their ends to the card stock's back surface.

13 Position the paste-paper book cover face up. Using the crease lines on the cover as guides, glue the watercolor paper to its front surface. Then glue the crimped card stock to the watercolor paper and the large embossed motif to the crimped card stock.

Tip

- To make a *prairie point*, first fold a square piece of card stock in half to form a rectangle. Place the rectangle on your work surface, with its short ends facing to the left and right, and the fold at the top. Then bend each top corner down to the center of the bottom edge, so the two corners meet. Voila! A quaint little point to add to this or to any other project.

The Bookmark

1 Cut a 6" x 8" piece of paste paper. Fold its long edges to the back and overlap them by ½", so that the front of the folded rectangle is 3½" wide. Glue the overlapping flaps together.

2 Tear out a 3" x 5½" rectangle of white watercolor paper. Center this on the front of the bookmark and glue it in place. Then cut a 2½" x 4½" piece of crimped taupe card stock; center it on the white watercolor paper and glue it in place.

3 Emboss four small corner motifs on aqua card stock; then trim around them to create triangles that measure about ⅝" x ⅝" x 1". Glue these onto pieces of purple card stock and trim the purple card stock to leave a ⅛"-wide purple border around each aqua triangle. Then glue one layered triangle to each corner of the crimped card stock, as shown in the project photo.

4 Repeat step 4 on page 50 to create another aqua-and-purple layered square.

5 Cut six 12" lengths of floss and eight 12" strands of metallic thread. Knot them together 1" from their ends to create a tassel. Knot them again about 4" below the first knot. String a five-bead set onto four of the tassel's metallic threads, as shown in the project photo, knotting each thread to prevent the beads from shifting.

6 Glue the tassel to the back of the embossed square so that one knot is above one corner of the square and the other knot is below the opposite corner.

7 Center the square, face up, on the crimped card stock, letting the tassel threads hang freely below the lower edge of the bookmark. Glue the square in place and trim the thread ends as desired.

Embossed Luminaria

Who needs a starry evening when this dreamy, twilight-blue luminaria can twinkle at you instead? Embossed stars and translucent vellum replace the night in this simple yet elegant lantern.

1 Cut off the top of the carton to make it about 6½" tall.

2 Spread a thin layer of craft glue over the carton's exterior. To wrap the carton with the 8½"-wide strip of art paper, position one short edge of the paper over one long edge of the carton, with an overlap of about ¾". Leave a 1" paper border at the top and a 1" border at the bottom. Press down the paper overlap; then bend the rest of the paper around the carton. As you work, fold the top border over to the carton's interior and glue it in place. Also fold the lower border down over the carton's base and glue it down. Press the paper down as you attach it, to remove wrinkles or air bubbles. If needed, trim the paper's vertical edge as you finish; its vertical seam—where it covers the ¾"-wide overlap—should be about ⅛" from the carton's vertical edge.

3 Using a large watercolor brush, color the paper-wrapped carton and the 3¼"-square piece of art paper with the blue and purple paints, diluting the paints with plenty of water to obtain the cloudy effect seen here. When the paper has dried, center the 3¼"-square piece on the bottom of the carton and glue it in place.

4 Using a pencil and the star templates, trace star images on the carton's panels. Then, using a sharp craft knife, carefully and slowly cut out each star shape, slicing through the painted paper and the carton beneath. Outline each hole with the silver metallic pen.

5 Cut out a piece of watercolor paper that is somewhat larger than one of the star templates; use the template to wet emboss the paper. (To ensure that the embossed edges will show through the carton's star cutout, use a template that is about ¼" smaller than the cutout's opening.) Repeat this step to make enough embossings to fill as many cutouts as you wish.

6 When the stars have dried, use craft glue or a glue gun to attach them to the inside of the carton, with their raised surfaces facing outward and showing through the cutouts.

7 Cut out several small pieces of vellum and glue them to the inside of the carton to cover the remaining holes.

8 Paint the dowels or pencils with the metallic or high-gloss paint and let them dry. Attach these to the carton's corners with a glue gun.

9 With the wire cutter, cut four 2" lengths of the wire and wrap them around the protruding tops of the dowels or pencils. Trim off any excess wire.

10 Cut four short lengths of metallic thread or floss. String and knot four or five decorative beads onto each strand. Then wrap the beaded strands around the dowel or pencil tops. Knot the strands and snip off any excess.

11 Place a votive candle or tea light inside the luminaria. To avoid fires, the user should keep an eye on the lantern when it's in use and not let the candle burn down too far.

MATERIALS AND TOOLS

Wet-embossing tools and supplies (see pages 10–11)

Empty cardboard milk or juice carton, each side about 3¾" wide

Medium-weight white art paper, 8½" x 16"

Medium-weight white art paper, 3¼" x 3¼"

Heavyweight white watercolor paper, 10" x 12"

Purple translucent vellum, 5" x 7"

Watercolor, gouache, or acrylic paints, in assorted shades of blue and purple

Several purchased or homemade star-shaped templates in a range of sizes that vary by about ¼" in diameter

Dark silver metallic ink pen

Dark silver metallic or high-gloss acrylic paint

Four wooden dowels, 5/16" in diameter, or pencils without erasers, each 7¼" long

Thin metal wire, 8" to 10" long

Wire cutter

Large watercolor brush

Silver metallic thread or embroidery thread, 8" to 10" long

Small, iridescent, multicolored beads, about 20

Votive candle or tea light

BASIC TECHNIQUES

Wet embossing (see pages 10–11)

Three-dimensional decorations (see page 35)

Maple Leaf Booklet

Autumn is often a time for contemplation. Help a friend capture his or her thoughts on paper with this small, pretty booklet that conjures up memories of crisp mornings and sweet maple syrup.

1 Place the white vellum on top of a piece of scrap paper that is larger than the vellum itself. Apply the palest ink pad directly to the vellum, lightly swirling the pad over it until you've colored the entire surface. (Let the color bleed off the edges.) Then, working from light to dark, swirl the other ink pads over the vellum, applying color randomly to create a cloud-like effect.

2 Trace the outline of the maple leaf onto the transparent vellum; then cut out the image with a craft knife.

3 Using the maple-leaf vellum stencil and the ink pads, stencil leaf images directly onto the paper. Allow the colors below to show through, and let some stenciled images bleed off the edges of the vellum. When the inks have dried, fold the vellum in half to create a journal cover that measures 4¼" x 5½".

4 Cut the two sheets of stationery paper in half to create four 5½" x 8½" sheets. Then fold these sheets in half to form eight 4¼" x 5½" journal pages. Stencil a leaf image onto each right-hand page, using one or more of the colors that you used on the cover, and running some of the images off the edges of the pages. Let the inks dry.

5 Place the folded pages inside the folded cover. Using a large needle, carefully punch a hole through the pages and spine of the journal, 1" from the top of the journal. Repeat to punch a second hole 1" from the bottom. Be sure to keep the pages aligned as you do this.

6 Thread the needle with a length of floss or thread. Then use the needle to thread the strand into the lower hole (from the outside of the journal) and out again through the upper hole. Let a few inches of thread extend from each hole. Repeat this process with as many strands as desired, being careful not to dislodge any previously threaded strands.

7 Thread several beads onto one of the thicker strands extending from the lower hole. Then bring all the lower strands up to the threads hanging from the upper hole and, holding them taut, tie the two groups of threads together. Trim the tail of this bundle as desired.

8 Thread a few beads onto some of the strands in the tail, knotting the threads firmly to hold the beads in place.

MATERIALS AND TOOLS

Stamping tools and supplies (see pages 15–18)

Stenciling tools and supplies (see pages 33–34)

Heavyweight white vellum paper, 5½" x 8½"

Heavyweight transparent vellum, 6" x 6"

Flecked stationery paper: two sheets, each 8½" x 11"

Parchment, yellow, lime green, spring green, and apricot pigment-ink stamp pads (raised or removable; see "Tip," page 91)

Assorted rayon, silk, and metallic threads and embroidery floss, each 12" long

Assorted seed and bugle beads in coordinating colors

Small maple leaf

Large needle

BASIC TECHNIQUES

Stenciling (see pages 33–34)

Folding (see "Tips," page 32)

Three-dimensional decorations (see page 35)

Batik Frame

This colorful frame owes its decidedly modern look to a surprising source: the ancient art of batik. In this Indonesian hand-printing method, alternating layers of hot wax and liquid dye are applied to fabric. The wax serves as a resist to protect the covered areas from the dyes. In this project, you'll apply only one layer of wax—to paper.

Note: If you use the frame kit (see "Materials and Tools") rather than making a frame from scratch, omit steps 5, 6, 10, and 11.

1 Melt the wax in the double boiler over the heating element; don't let it smoke or burn.

2 Place the mulberry paper on several sheets of clean newsprint. Dip a medium-sized watercolor brush into the hot wax and spatter it over the paper by gently shaking the brush. (Wear gloves and protective eye shields, and make sure your work space is ventilated.) Let the wax cool and harden.

3 Mix the dyes according to the manufacturer's instructions and dilute them to the desired intensity. Using the watercolor brush, brush various dyes across the paper's surface with broad, sweeping motions (refer to the project photo for placement). To avoid mixing hues, rinse the brush thoroughly between color applications.

4 To remove the wax, place the decorated paper between two thick layers of newsprint and use a warm iron to press the upper layer. The newsprint will pick up the wax. Repeat, using clean newsprint each time, until the decorated paper is free of wax.

5 To make the frame, first cut a 3"-square opening in the center of one piece of binder's board, to make a frame shape with 2"-wide borders. Cut 3½"-square openings in the other boards, centering each hole. (Save the cutouts.)

6 Stack and glue the boards together, placing the board with the 3"-square opening on top. Set them under heavy weights until the glue has dried.

7 Place the decorated paper right side down on your work surface. Coat the back with spray adhesive and center the frame on top of it, with the frame's smaller opening face down. Turn the frame over and smooth the paper onto its front face, leaving a paper border all the way around.

8 Using a craft knife, cut away the paper that covers the frame's opening, leaving interior borders of paper about 1" wide. Slice four diagonal slits in the paper, from each inner corner to an inner corner of the frame.

9 Wrap the inner paper borders around the frame's inner edges and glue them in place, smoothing down all surfaces with a bone folder, including the layered edges around the frame's opening. Fold the outer paper borders over the outer edges of the frame, trim them as necessary, and glue them to the back of the frame.

10 Trim a 3½"-square binder's board cutout (see step 5) to fit in the opening in the back of the frame. Cover it with decorated paper if you like.

11 Fasten the picture-hanging clip to the frame's back and insert a swing clip at each edge of the opening.

12 Without turning the frame over, place the glass or acrylic in the frame opening, followed by the picture you wish to display. Insert the frame back and turn the clips to hold the pieces in place.

MATERIALS AND TOOLS

- White mulberry paper, about 16" x 20"
- Clean newsprint, several sheets
- Wax (batik wax, beeswax, or paraffin)
- Double boiler
- Heating element (stove or hot plate)
- Medium-sized watercolor brush
- Protective gloves
- Eye shields
- Orange, green, dark blue, and purple fabric dyes or batik dyes
- Iron
- Ironing board
- Magenta frame kit #SPF or
  - Binder's board: four pieces, each 7" x 7"
  - Utility knife
  - Heavy weights, such as books or bricks
- Window glass or acrylic, 3⅜" square
- Four swing clips (also called "turn buttons") and screws for frame back
- Picture-hanging clip and screw

BASIC TECHNIQUE

Folding (see "Tips," page 32)

Stamped Coasters

It's party time! Treat the hostess to these truly distinctive coasters; you know she'll invite you back to enjoy them again and again. And while you're at it, why not make a few for yourself?

Terra-Cotta and Lavender Coasters

1 Apply background colors to the coasters by gently stroking the terra-cotta and blue-lavender ink pads directly against the paper. Color the coasters' edges with the blue-lavender ink pad. (You may want to round off the coasters' corners with a pair of scissors before applying colors.)

2 Using the terra-cotta pad, ink a blender stylus tip (the "clover" tip was used here), and stamp nine solid images onto each coaster, positioning them as shown in the photo.

3 Soften a moldable stylus tip with heat from a light bulb. Then press the tip against the portion of the floral motif stamp to mold it. Let the tip cool and harden.

4 Using the purple ink, ink the molded stylus tip and stamp the floral motif on top of the previously printed shapes.

5 Using the sphere stamp and purple ink, stamp images in the spaces between the floral designs. Then cover the entire surface of each coaster using the lines and small dots stamp and the blue-lavender ink.

6 Heat-set the pigment inks with a craft heat gun, following the manufacturer's instructions.

Tip

- The designs on these coasters were created with a special stylus (available from many craft and rubber-stamp stores) that is used with moldable tips. If you don't have access to this tool, either use the stamps recommended in the "Materials and Tools" list, masking them (see page 20) to expose only the desired portions of the designs, or select and use any stamps you like.

Terra-Cotta and Turquoise Coasters

1 Apply the turquoise and terra-cotta background colors to the coasters by gently stroking the ink pads directly against the paper. Color the coasters' edges with the turquoise ink pad.

2 Mold two, diamond-shaped stylus tips, using one or more portions of the leaves and swirled floral stamp. If you have only one diamond-shaped stylus tip, mold one image and stamp it; then reheat and remold the tip, and stamp the other image.

3 Ink the molded stylus tips with the turquoise and terra-cotta inks and stamp images on the coasters, using the project photo as your guide. Stamp an occasional purple image, as well, for variety.

4 Heat-set the pigment inks with a craft heat gun, following the manufacturer's instructions.

MATERIALS AND TOOLS

Stamping tools and supplies (see pages 15–18)

Heat-embossing tools and supplies (see pages 11–13)

Paper coasters (Magenta, #CSS) or several 3¼"-square pieces of heavy-weight bristol board

Purple, terra-cotta, turquoise, and blue-lavender pigment-ink stamp pads (raised or removable; see "Tip," page 91)

ColorToolBox Stylus Tray (Clearsnap, #69004)

Leaves and swirled floral stamp (Magenta, #20.016.P)

Floral motif stamp (Magenta, #14.107.F)

Lines and small dots stamp (Magenta, #I-0228)

Sphere stamp (Magenta, #21.036.B)

BASIC TECHNIQUES

Stamping (see pages 14–21)

Heat embossing (see pages 11–13)

Paste-Paper Journal

Any budding poet would appreciate receiving this lovely journal. The beautiful design and richly textured paper are sure to inspire a rhyme or two.

1 Referring to figure 1, fold one sheet of paper in half and tear it along the fold line to create two 20" x 25" pieces. Fold each of these sheets in half and tear each one along its fold line to create four 10" x 25" sheets. Set one of these aside to serve as the cover. Fold and tear the remaining three 10" x 25" sheets in half to create six 10" x 12½" pieces. Then fold these pieces in half again—but don't tear them apart—to form 6¼" x 10" text pages.

2 Fold and tear the remaining 25" x 40" piece of paper to make more 6¼" x 10" text pages. You should now have a total of fourteen folded text pages.

3 Place each folded text page inside the next to form a signature (this book-related term refers to one set of pages). Either leave the edges rough for an attractive deckle edge or trim them with a paper cutter or a craft knife and ruler.

4 Fold the piece of paper that you set aside as the cover (see step 1) in half and crease the fold line. Tuck the signature into the folded cover, pressing its folded edges tightly against the cover's fold. Using figure 2 (see page 62) as a guide, make a light pencil mark on the cover, about 1⁄16" beyond the front edge of the signature pages. Then fold the cover along this line, back inside toward the spine, to create a flap. Now measure the distance between this fold and the cover's folded spine, and make another mark on the back cover that is the same distance from the spine. Fold the back cover in the same fashion.

5 Prepare your paste using your favorite recipe. Color one container of paste with the gold paint and another with the purple paint.

6 Moisten the cover sheet with water and use a sponge to smooth it down onto your work surface. Using the broad edge of the turquoise pastel stick, make random marks all over the paper.

7 Cover the entire surface of the paper with the gold paste, letting the pastel bleed into the gold pigment to create blue-green hues. Comb wavy vertical lines across the paper with the serrated

Figure 1

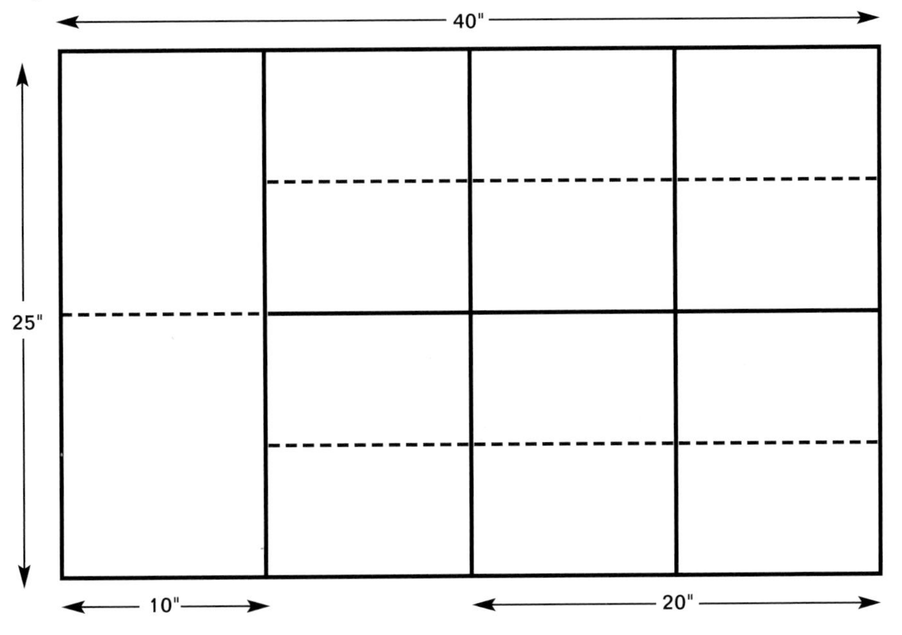

MATERIALS AND TOOLS

Paste-paper tools, supplies, and recipes (see pages 23–25 and step 7)

175-pound, 100% cotton, white text wove paper: two sheets, each 25" x 40"

Purple and gold acrylic paints

Turquoise pastel stick

Combing tool (plastic paint scraper or cardboard notched at ¼" intervals)

One sheet of thin acetate, 9" x 12"

Pinking shears

Linen thread, 30" long

Large sewing needle

Beeswax or white candle

Two large beads or buttons

Newsprint or other thick material to use as a blotter

BASIC TECHNIQUES

Paste paper (see pages 22–29)

Folding (see "Tips," page 32)

Three-dimensional decorations (see page 35)

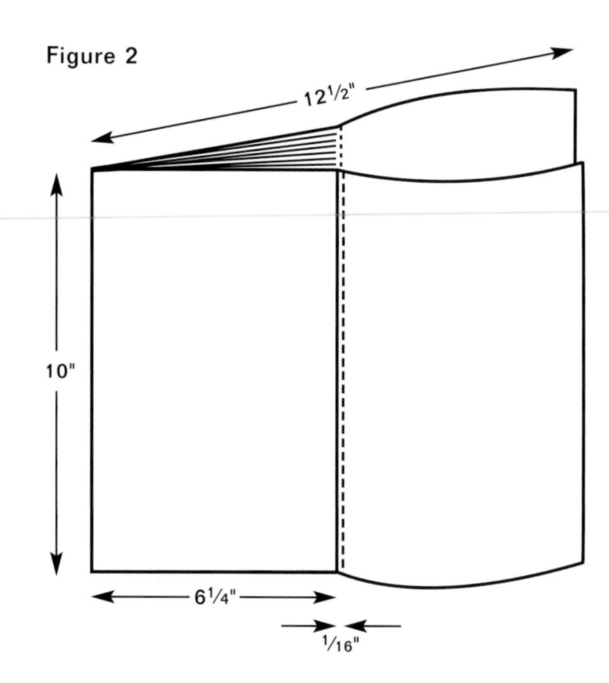

scraper or piece of cardboard, overlapping your strokes in some areas.

8 Using pinking shears, cut the sheet of acetate into four pieces, each measuring 4" x 5½". (Experiment with other shapes, too, if you like.) Position each piece on the cover as desired and tap on them lightly to press them into the paste.

9 Paint the entire surface of the cover with the purple paste, letting it blend with the gold paste. Comb another set of wavy vertical lines on the paper, scraping over the pieces of plastic as if they weren't there.

10 Carefully remove each sheet of acetate by first lifting up a corner with a thin, pointed instrument such as a needle or scraper. Use the same method to lift the cover paper off the work surface. Discard the acetate and dry the paper on a blotter for several hours.

11 After the cover has dried, refold it along the spine and along the two flap lines. Place the loose text pages inside, pressing their folds against the spine. Open the pages to the center.

12 Holding the pages firmly in place, poke a needle through all the pages and the cover, at the center of the fold line. Then poke two more holes, approximately 1" from the top and 1" from the bottom of the book.

13 Cut a 30" piece of linen thread and wax it by running it across the beeswax or candle. (This prevents kinking and helps to hold the knots securely.) Thread the needle and leave it unknotted (let a few inches of thread trail from the needle's eye).

14 Run the threaded needle through the outside center hole to the inside of the booklet, leaving several inches of thread outside the cover. Then bring the needle and thread up and out through the top hole, down the spine and in through the bottom hole.

15 Bring the threaded needle back out through the center hole, remove the needle, and trim the two thread ends to equal lengths. Tie the thread ends together at the center hole. Then thread a bead onto each strand and tie knots in the thread to keep the beads from sliding off.

Tip

As you can see in the project photo, the designer of this journal included a sheet of hand-dyed paper between the text pages and the cover. If you'd like to add similar endpapers to your journal, simply add a folded piece of colored paper to your text pages.

Holiday Gift Tags and Stickers

There won't be a present left under the tree after people reach for these beautiful gift tags and stickers. Amid the "oohs" and "aahs" exclaimed over these little delights, people may actually forget to open their gifts!

MATERIALS AND TOOLS

Stamping tools and supplies (see pages 15–18)

Heat-embossing tools and supplies (see pages 11–13)

Bright red paper, 6" x 6"

Green card stock, 6" x 6"

Striped printed paper, 1¾" x 1¾"

Dark red cover stock, 6" x 10"

Gold foil paper, 6" x 8"

Red wave-corrugated cover stock, 6" x 6"

White ink stamp pad

Embossing-ink stamp pad

Gold embossing powder

Gold metallic ink pen

Spiral stamp (Hero Arts, #A1294)

Bold leaves stamp (Hero Arts, #E1529)

Aspen stamp (Hero Arts, #E1527)

Leaf stamp (DeNami Design, #G83)

Fall leaf stamp (Judi-Kins, #6557H)

Squares stamp and star stamp (All Night Media, Doodles, #2908Q)

Large circle hole punch

BASIC TECHNIQUES

Stamping (see pages 14–21)

Heat embossing (see pages 11–13)

Folding (see "Tips," page 32)

Layering paper (see page 32)

White Swirls Tag

1 Using the white ink pad, stamp the spiral image on a portion of the bright red paper. Cut out a 1¼"-square piece from the stamped area.

2 Cut out a 1½"-square piece of green card stock. Center the stamped square on top of it and glue the two pieces together. Center the glued pieces on the square of striped printed paper and glue them in place.

3 Cut a 2¼" x 4½" piece of dark red cover stock and fold it in half to make a 2¼"-square tag. Center the layered squares on the tag and glue them in place.

Square-Stamped Tag

1 Using embossing ink and the squares stamp, stamp an image on the bright red paper. Emboss the image using the gold embossing powder and then cut out a 1"-square piece from the embossed area.

2 Cut a 1⅜"-square piece of green card stock. Center the embossed square on it and glue it in place.

3 Cut a 1⅞" x 5¼" piece of dark red cover stock and fold it in half to make a 1⅞" x 2⅝" tag. Center the layered papers on the tag and glue them in place.

4 Using the gold metallic pen, outline the four edges of the green square and draw small dots in the centers of some of the embossed squares.

Three-Leaf Tag

1 Using the bold leaves stamp (which has five leaves on it) and embossing ink, stamp leaves on the remaining green card stock. Emboss the images using gold embossing powder; then cut out each leaf.

2 Cut a 1 3/4" x 2 3/8" piece of the red corrugated cover paper and a 2" x 2 5/8" piece of gold foil paper. Using the photo as a guide, glue three of the leaf cutouts to the corrugated paper. (Save the two remaining leaves to use as decorative stickers or to embellish other projects.) Center the corrugated paper on the gold foil paper and glue it in place.

3 Cut a 3 1/8" x 4 3/4" piece of dark red cover stock and fold it in half to make a 2 3/8" x 3 1/8" tag. Center the layered papers on the tag and glue them in place.

4 Cut a 2 3/8" x 5" piece of dark red cover stock and fold it in half to make a 2 3/8" x 2 1/2" tag. Center the layered papers on the tag and glue them in place.

5 Using the gold metallic pen, color the recessed areas on the corrugated paper inside the circle.

Tip

- Wave-corrugated cover paper is available at art-supply stores, but you may corrugate your own with a paper crimper if you like. Many craft stores sell bags of assorted decorative papers, which sometimes include sheets of crimped paper.

Circle Tag

1 Punch a 7/8"-diameter circle through a portion of the remaining gold foil paper. Then cut out a 1 3/8"-square piece of this paper, with the circle in its center.

2 Cut out a 1 7/8" x 2" piece of red corrugated cover paper. Center the gold hole-punched paper on the corrugated paper and glue it in place.

3 Cut a 2 1/8" x 2 1/4" piece of gold foil paper. Center the layered pieces on the gold foil paper and glue them in place.

Holiday Stickers

1 Using embossing ink and the various leaf and patterned stamps, stamp several images on the bright red paper and green card stock.

2 Emboss the images using the gold embossing powder. After they have cooled, cut them out. To use the stickers, simply glue them in place with a glue stick.

Framing Mats

If pictures are worth a thousand words, the beautiful mats surrounding them must be worth a million. And you'll feel like a million (bucks, that is) when you present these lovely gifts. So cook up some paste and get out your favorite tools for this project. The results will look great in anyone's home or office.

1 Prepare several coordinating sheets of paste paper using your favorite paste recipe and colors. The papers shown were made using a cornstarch recipe. The artist colored her pastes various shades of green, red, and turquoise, and she mixed ultrafine glitter into some of the pastes to provide subtle luster. She brushed and combed the turquoise paste paper and the small green mat shown here. One sheet of light red paper was brushed and then stamped with the decorative scroll stamp. On the other red and green papers, the artist used serrated weather stripping to create allover patterns, combing her lines and waves in multiple directions. She also swirled a fingertip over the olive green paper to create the arches that sweep across the horizontal and vertical lines beneath.

2 Cut a piece of paste paper 2" wider and 2" longer than the mat you want to cover. Place the paper right side down on your work surface and coat the back with spray adhesive.

3 Lay the mat face down on top of the paper's adhesive surface and smooth it down completely, leaving a 2" paste-paper border all the way around.

4 Using a craft knife, cut out the paste paper that covers the mat's opening, leaving a ½"-wide inner border around all four of the opening's sides. Slit the four corners of this inner paste-paper border at 45-degree angles, from the corner of the paper to the corner of the mat.

5 With a pair of scissors, cut off the tip of each outer paste-paper corner at a 45-degree angle, making these cuts just short of the mat's outer corner.

6 Fold the top and bottom edges of the outer paper border over the outer edges of the mat. To make sure the paper is tight against the mat, press the materials firmly against a table or other hard work surface.

7 Fold down the paper borders along the sides, making a little tuck at each corner before smoothing the paper down.

8 Wrap the inner paper borders around the mat's inner edges. Smooth down all surfaces with a bone folder, including the beveled edges around the mat's opening.

9 Repeat this process for as many mats as you'd like to cover. Consider layering two or three paste-paper mats in a frame and separating them with plain precut mats in contrasting colors.

Tip

- Glue your paste-paper creations to ready-made mats. These come in a variety of standard sizes, ensuring that your handiwork will fit in standard-size frames and saving you the trouble of trying to cut perfectly beveled edges from a solid piece of mat board (which is no easy feat).

MATERIALS AND TOOLS

Paste-paper tools, supplies, and recipes (see pages 23–25 and step 1)

75-pound classic laid text paper, several sheets

Acrylic paints in assorted colors

Decorative scroll stamp (Rubber Stampede, #61023)

Serrated weather stripping

Ready-made, precut mats, various sizes

Ready-made frames, various sizes

BASIC TECHNIQUES

Stamping (see pages 14–21)

Paste paper (see pages 22–29)

Accordion-Fold Journal

Friends will cherish this oriental-style memento. Decorative papers of assorted colors and weights, some gracefully feathered, are layered to provide depth and texture to the cover. Dry embossing and a single fern frond add subtlety and refinement.

1 To begin each of the covers, center a piece of the binder's board on one of the two larger pieces of deep orange paper. Fold the edges of the paper up and onto the top of the board and glue the paper down with craft glue. Repeat this process with the other piece of binder's board and sheet of deep orange paper. Set the two covers aside.

2 Dry emboss the white kochi paper. The paper shown in the project photo was burnished over a hand-carved woodblock, but any raised embossing template (or object that can serve as one) will do. Kochi is very soft and thick, so you must apply a lot of pressure when burnishing the surface to make the relief stand out. To avoid tearing the paper, burnish firmly but very carefully. When you're finished, cut out a 1⅝" x 3" rectangle from the embossed paper.

3 Highlight the raised areas of the embossed design by rubbing them lightly with a very sharp, lime green colored pencil. Be gentle; add just a hint of color.

4 Tear the yellow and green decorative papers to form asymmetrical shapes, each somewhat larger than the fern frond.

5 Glue five layers of paper to the front cover, positioning them as shown in the project photo, and attaching them in the following order: the purple paper, the red paper, the embossed kochi paper, the torn green paper, and the torn yellow paper. (If your papers are very thin, use spray mount adhesive instead of glue.) Glue the fern frond to the yellow paper.

6 Using the colored pencil, outline the embossed paper and the red paper to add emphasis and to tie the design elements together visually.

7 Place the drawing paper or bristol board on your work surface, with its short ends facing left and right. Measure and mark a point every 3" along the top of the paper. (Make very light pencil marks as you do this.) Then create the accordion pages by folding the paper at each pair of marks. Use a bone folder to burnish each fold.

8 Glue the ribbon across the width of the inside back cover, letting the ends trail out from the cover's sides.

9 Glue the back panel of the accordion-folded paper to the inside of the back cover, with the folded edge of the panel on the left-hand side of the cover. Repeat to glue the front panel to the inside of the front cover, with the panel's folded edge on the cover's right-hand side.

MATERIALS AND TOOLS

Dry-embossing tools and supplies (see pages 7–9)

Binder's board or heavyweight mat board: two pieces, each 3¼" x 4¾"

Heavyweight drawing paper or bristol board, 4½" x 18"

Deep orange oriental decorative paper with golden threads: two sheets, each 4¼" x 5¾"

White kochi paper, 2" x 4"

Purple oriental decorative paper, 2¾" x 4½"

Red oriental decorative paper, 2" x 3½"

Green oriental decorative paper, 2" x 3"

Yellow oriental decorative paper, 2" x 3"

Narrow red satin ribbon, 24" long

Lime green colored pencil

Dried fern frond

BASIC TECHNIQUES

Dry embossing (see pages 7–9)

Folding (see "Tips," page 32)

Layering paper (see page 32)

Creating decorative edges (see page 31)

Three-dimensional decorations (see page 35)

Stamped Paste-Paper Mirror

Look! There's a monkey swinging from the sinuous vines on this mirror frame. Cleverly chosen stamps transform an abstract paste-paper design into an engaging jungle.

1 Create a sheet of paste paper using your favorite recipe (a mixed-flours paste was used in this project). Color the paste with brown acrylic paint and cover the watercolor paper with it. Use a rubber wedge tool to form the knotted, linear patterns and the edge of a plastic credit card to create the sharply combed, angled lines. Let the paper dry.

2 To create a frame, cut a 6" x 6" opening in the center of one of the heavy poster boards.

3 Apply glue to the surface of the frame; then center the paste paper over the frame and press it down to secure it, leaving a 1½"-wide border around the frame's perimeter.

Tip

- If you like, you may display this mirror on a large plate stand. To hang it on a wall, first use a silicone caulk to attach two flat metal picture frame hooks (available at frame shops) to the poster-board backing. (Select a caulk that will form a very strong bond on both porous and non-porous surfaces.) Then loop picture-hanging wire through the hooks and hang the mirror from a picture-hanging hook and nail.

4 Using a craft knife, cut a large "X" in the center of the paste paper, through the hole in the poster-board frame. Fold the triangular sections of cut paper through the hole and glue them to the back of the frame.

5 Turn the frame over, center the mirror tile on its back, and glue it to the frame with silicone adhesive. Glue the other poster board on top of it, aligning its edges with the edges of the frame.

6 Fold the paste-paper borders to the back of the poster board and glue them to it.

7 Pour a small amount of the black stamping paint onto a palette or foam plate. Load the flat edge of a wedge sponge with this paint and pat the paint onto the surface of the monkey stamp. Stamp the monkey onto the upper left-hand portion of the frame. Clean the stamp with water.

8 Coat the leaf grass stamp with the bright green stamping paint, just as you did in step 7. Stamp a couple of images onto the upper left-hand portion of the frame and onto the lower right-hand corner. Recoat the stamp after each printing. Clean the stamp.

9 Coat the leaf grass stamp with the dark green stamping paint and overlap the previously stamped leaves, again reapplying paint between stampings. Clean the stamp and let the paper dry.

MATERIALS AND TOOLS

Paste-paper tools, supplies, and recipes (see pages 23–25 and step 1)

Stamping tools and supplies (see pages 15–18)

White watercolor paper, 15½" x 15½"

Heavy poster board: two pieces, each 14" x 14"

Brown acrylic paint

Rubber wedge tool

Plastic credit card

Mirror tile, 12" x 12" (available at hardware stores)

Silicone adhesive

Black, bright green, and dark green stamping paints

Leaf grass stamp (Rubber Stampede, #72125)

Monkey stamp (Rubber Stampede, #72123)

BASIC TECHNIQUES

Stamping (see pages 14–21)

Paste paper (see pages 22–29)

Greeting Card and Envelope

Banish the blues with this cheery card and envelope; the cherries practically pop off the card and into your mouth. Layered papers and some artful coloring set off the simple, stamped centerpiece, and raising the centerpiece above the card's surface adds dimension. The lucky recipient will soon agree that life's a bowl of cherries.

The Card

1 Feather the edges of the beige handmade paper, center the paper on the persimmon-color card, and glue it in place. Set the card aside.

2 Ink the cherry stamp with the black ink and stamp the design onto the tan card stock. Let the ink dry.

3 Using the photo as a guide and working from light to dark, color the stamped cherry image with the water-soluble markers. Then, using a wet paintbrush, blend the colors a little. Let the colors dry.

4 Using the green, purple, and red markers, randomly color about one-third of the checkered paper, at one short end of the 11" x 17" sheet. Let the colors overlap; then blend them a little by using the wet paintbrush. Set the paper aside to dry.

5 While the papers are drying, use the paper crimper to crimp the sage card stock.

6 Cut a 2" x 2½" rectangle from the black-and-white portion of the checkered paper. Then, from the colored portion, cut six ¾" x ¾" squares and a ¼" x 2½" strip. (You'll use three of the squares when you line the envelope.)

7 Using the photo as a guide, glue the crimped sage card stock to the handmade paper. Next, center the 2" x 2½" piece of checkered paper on the sage card stock and glue it in place. Then glue three of the colored checkered squares and the narrow, colored checkered strip to the beige paper.

8 Cut the stamped cherry image from the dried tan card stock. Remove the protective backing from one side of a self-adhesive foam dot and attach the dot to the back of the leaf; stick the other dot to the back of a cherry. Remove the remaining protective backings, position the cherries as shown in the photo, and press the dots into place on the card.

9 To create each of the thick strands for the buttons, twist together three 6" lengths of floss. Thread each button with one twisted strand and tie each strand off with a square knot at the button holes. Tie a couple of extra knots in the strands and trim the strands to the lengths shown in the photo. Then glue the buttons to the card.

The Envelope

1 Cut a 5¾" x 7¼" piece of the checkered paper. Slide the paper into the persimmon-color envelope until it touches bottom. Trim it to fit, leaving a ½"-wide strip of the envelope's adhesive area exposed at the top. Glue the liner to the inside of the envelope.

2 Glue the remaining three checkered squares to the liner as shown in the project photo.

MATERIALS AND TOOLS

Stamping tools and supplies (see pages 15–18)

Beige handmade paper, 3½" x 5¼"

Ready-made persimmon-color card, 4¼" x 5⅞"

Ready-made matching persimmon-color envelope, 4½" x 6"

Tan card stock, 4" x 4"

Black-and-white checkered paper, 11" x 17"

Sage green card stock, 3" x 3½" (not crimped)

Black ink stamp pad

Buttons

Lavender, red, and green embroidery floss

Yellow, red, brown, purple, and green water-soluble markers

Two double-sided, self-adhesive foam dots

Cherry stamp (Rubber Stampede, A225E)

Paper crimper

BASIC TECHNIQUES

Stamping (see pages 14–21)

Creating decorative edges (see page 31)

Crimping (see page 31)

Layering paper (see page 32)

Three-dimensional decorations (see page 35)

Stationery Folder

Letter writers will love this stunning yet practical stationery folder. Only 8 3/4" wide when folded, it will fit easily into a purse, briefcase, or backpack. Its sturdy back makes a nice little writing table, whether you're writing a letter on the subway, on your patio, or under a tree.

1 Prepare a sheet of paste paper, using the all-media paper and a mixed-flours paste. Color one container of paste green and another blue. Using a 3" foam paintbrush for each color, spread patches of the green and blue pastes over the paper, overlapping the colors in some areas. For more texture, use a bamboo brush to spatter additional blue and green paste over the surface. Press a large sheet of plastic wrap gently over the paper and scrunch the plastic between your fingers to wrinkle it in the paste. Remove the wrap after the paste has dried a bit but is still somewhat moist. Use a bamboo brush to spatter the copper metallic paint over the design. Set the paper aside to dry.

2 Cut two 4¼" x 6⅛" pieces of binder's board and one 6⅛" x 8½" piece. Cut three pieces of blotting paper in the same sizes. Set these materials aside.

3 Cut two 4⅝" x 7⅛" pieces of paste paper and one 7⅛" x 8⅛" piece. Set these aside.

4 Wrap the stack of ready-made stationery in waxed paper and tape the package shut. Divide the ready-made envelopes into two stacks, wrap them in waxed paper, and tape these packages shut, too.

5 Cut four 4" x 15" strips of paste paper. Fold a ¼" hem down each side of every strip. You'll use these strips to make the "pockets" into which the envelopes and stationery will fit. Using the photo (on the opposite page) as a guide, wrap one strip around one long edge of each package of envelopes and one strip around each short edge of the stationery package. Glue the overlapping ends and edge of each strip together.

6 To calculate the width of the folder's hinges, you'll make a stack of all the materials that will eventually make up the closed folder. Stack the following materials in this order: the large piece of binder's board, the stack of stationery wrapped in waxed paper and paste paper, one stack of wrapped envelopes, two pieces of paste paper, two pieces of blotting paper, and one of the smaller pieces of binder's board. Wrap this bundle with a long piece of scrap paper. Crease the scrap paper at the top and bottom edges of the stack. The distance between these creases is the width of each hinge. (If the hinges are too narrow, the case won't close properly, and if the hinges are too large, the folder's components will slide around.)

7 Iron the interfacing onto the back of the blue fabric, following the manufacturer's instructions. Now you'll cut two 6¾"-long strips from this

MATERIALS AND TOOLS

Paste-paper tools, supplies, and recipes (see pages 23–25 and step 1)

80-pound white all-media paper, 24" x 32"

Bright greenish blue, ultramarine blue, and copper metallic acrylic paints

Foam paintbrush, 3" wide

Bamboo brush

Plastic wrap

Binder's board or heavyweight mat board, 24" x 32"

Dark blue blotting paper, 18" x 24"

Ready-made stationery, 5⅝" x 7¾"

Ready-made matching envelopes, 4" x 5¾"

Waxed paper

Iron-on interfacing, ½ yard

Dark blue cotton fabric (preferably book cloth), ½ yard

Iron and ironing board

Dark blue, coarse-grain ribbon, ⅜" wide and 60" long

Weights (heavy books)

BASIC TECHNIQUES

Paste paper (see pages 22–29)

Spattering (see page 35)

Three-dimensional decorations (see page 35)

Figure 1

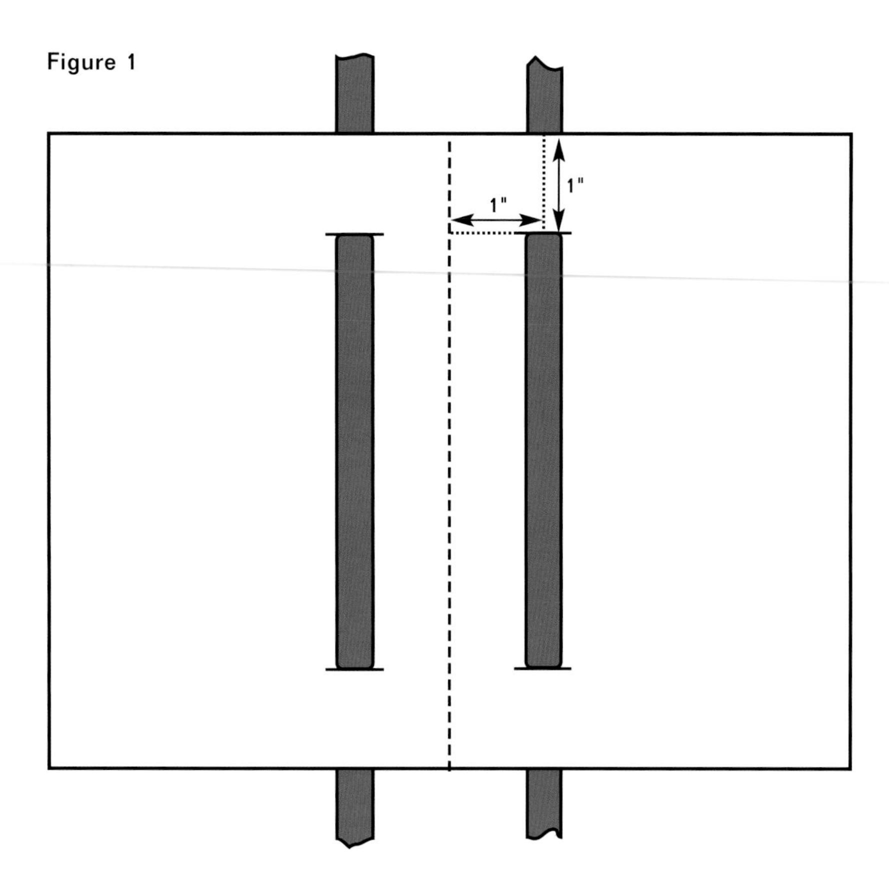

material, making sure that the long measurements are parallel to the fabric's selvage. To determine the width of each strip, add 1" to the hinge measurement determined in step 6. Cut these strips out. With a pencil, mark the hinge width down the center of each strip, on the interfacing side, leaving a $\frac{1}{2}$" border on each side.

8 Cut two pieces of blue fabric to line the hinges. Each piece should be $5\frac{3}{4}$" long and the same width that you calculated in step 7. Set all of the fabric aside.

9 Place the $6\frac{1}{8}$" x $8\frac{1}{2}$" piece of binder's board on your work surface, with its short ends facing left and right, and mark a line down its center. Next, using figure 1 as a guide, mark two parallel lines, 1" to the left and 1" to the right of the centerline. Mark two points on each of these two lines, 1" from the top of the board and 1" from the bottom. Using a craft knife, cut a $\frac{3}{8}$"-wide slit at each of the four marks.

10 Cut the ribbon in half and run each ribbon through the slits, leaving equal amounts of ribbon hanging from the ends of the board. Glue the ribbons to the slits on both sides of the board. Roll the ribbon ends up in plastic wrap to keep them clean during the folder's construction.

11 To attach the three binder's boards with the fabric hinges, first refer to figure 2, opposite. Then, using a straightedge as your guide, arrange the three pieces of binder's board on your work surface, ribbon side (or outside) facing up, with the large board in the center and the small boards on either side of it. Leave a gap (see step 6) between each small board and the large one. Brush glue onto the $\frac{1}{2}$"-wide borders of the two $6\frac{3}{4}$"-long fabric strips (on the interfacing side), leaving small sections at both the top and bottom ends without glue. Then join the large board to each small board with a fabric strip, pressing the glue-covered fabric borders against the edges of the boards. Rub these edges down well with a bone folder.

12 Glue the ends of the fabric hinges to the inner faces of the boards. Brush glue onto the two $5\frac{3}{4}$"-long fabric strips and glue them onto the exposed inner surfaces of the fabric hinges. Burnish the strips well with a bone folder and place the materials under weights to dry.

13 Glue a $4\frac{5}{8}$" x $7\frac{1}{8}$" sheet of paste paper to the outer surface of each of the smaller boards, making sure that one edge of each sheet covers the outer edge of a fabric hinge. Fold the other three edges of each sheet to the inner surface of the board and glue them down. Rub the paper down well.

14 To cover the large binder's board, first place the board with its outer (ribbon) side facing up. Then brush glue onto the back of the $7\frac{1}{8}$" x $8\frac{1}{8}$" piece of paste paper and glue the paper to the outer surface of the board, leaving $\frac{1}{2}$" paper borders beyond the board's outermost

Figure 2

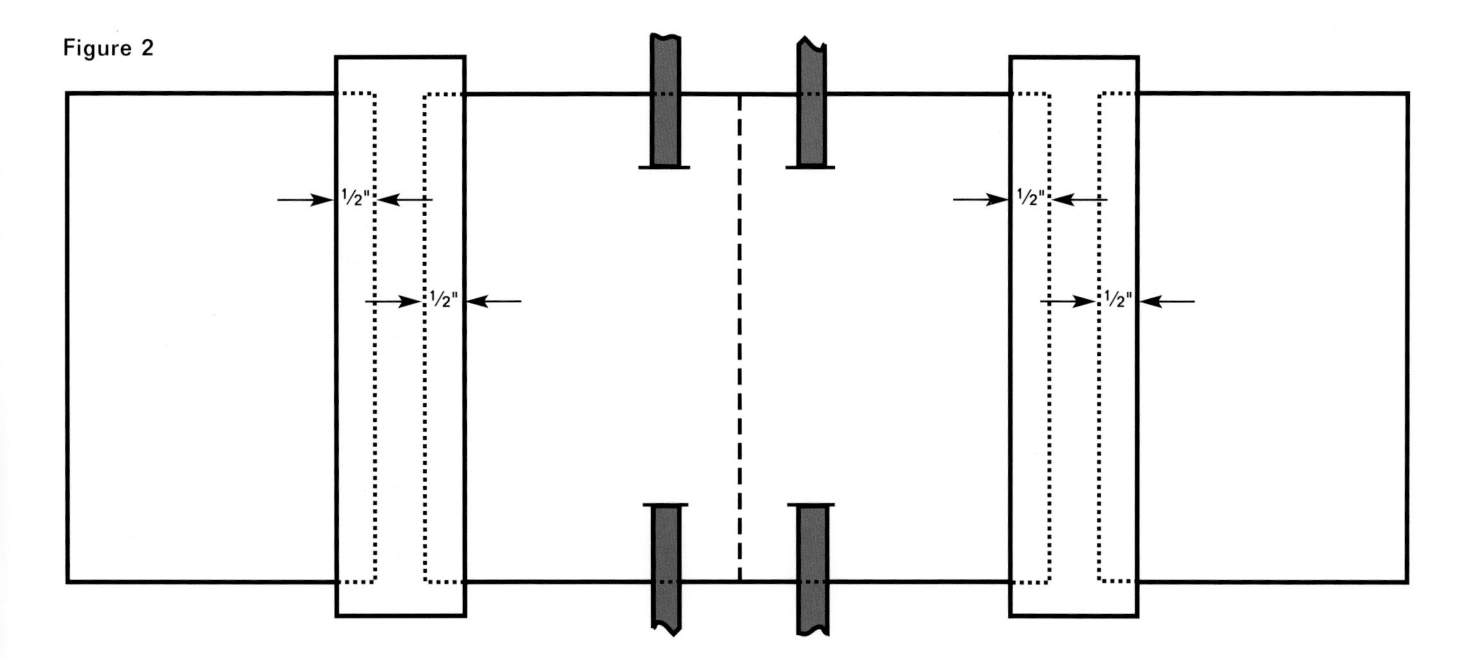

top and bottom edges. (Don't glue these borders down yet.) The right and left edges of the paste paper should cover the inner edges of the two fabric hinges. Rub the paper down well and place the materials under weights to dry.

- Iron-on interfacing is used here to prevent glue from seeping through the fabric hinges and staining them. An alternative way to protect the fabric is to coat some paper with craft glue and let the glue dry thoroughly. Place the fabric wrong side down on the dried glue surface and iron the pieces until they stick together, using the iron's wool setting.

15 Using a craft knife, cut four slits in the sheet of paste paper glued to the large board, two right at the board's top and two at the board's bottom where the ribbons will emerge. Unwrap the ribbons and pull them through these four slits. Now fold over the top and bottom borders of the paste paper and glue them in place on the inner face of the large binder's board. Rub the paper down well and once again place the materials under weights to dry.

16 With the wrapped envelopes still inside them, glue the envelope pockets to the inner surfaces of the smaller binder's boards. The pockets should open inward and should be attached about 1/8" in from the outer edges of the boards. Press the pockets into place. Then remove the waxed-paper packages and use a bone folder to rub the pockets down against the boards.

17 With the wrapped stationery still inside its pockets, repeat step 16 to glue the two pockets to the inside of the large binder's board. Leave a 1/8" gap between the side, top, and bottom edges of the board, and press the pockets into place. Remove the wrapped bundle and rub the pockets down well with a bone folder to secure them.

18 Trim the pieces of blotting paper to fit inside the pockets; then tuck them into the pockets. Glue the pockets and blotting papers to the inner faces of the assembled boards and rub them down well. Fit the waxed-paper packages back into their pockets and close the folder. Weight the closed folder lightly until the glue has dried.

19 Remove the waxed-paper packages, unwrap them, and insert the stationery and envelopes into their pockets. To hold the folder closed, just tie the ribbons around it.

Jewelry Box

This dazzling jewelry box can hold a treasure trove and will look lovely on a dresser or bedside table. Embellish your own version with assorted trinkets or with family mementos—perhaps a costume brooch that belonged to your grandmother or buttons saved from a child's special clothing.

1 Choose a stiff cardboard box for this project. You may use any size; just adapt the paper sizes and ribbon lengths as necessary.

2 Glue the green mulberry paper to the box and lid, covering the entire outer surface of each. (Leave a ½" border on all sides when cutting the paper to fit. Fold over these borders and glue them to the inner surfaces of the box and lid.)

3 Dampen the beige mulberry paper with water and tear it into 3" x 4" pieces. Gather enough pieces to cover the lid and then stamp fern images on them with the green ink.

4 Using a small art brush, spread craft glue over the lid. Press the stamped pieces of paper onto the lid in a random pattern, allowing the pieces to overlap slightly. As the wet glue moistens the water-based dye ink, the stamped images will bleed, taking on an attractive, water-stained look. Let the materials dry.

5 Spread glue over the box and cover the surface with the unstamped pieces of beige paper. Let the glue dry.

6 Using the embossing ink and gold embossing powder, stamp ferns over each previously stamped image on the lid and heat emboss them. Let the images cool.

7 Cut the gold ribbon into three equal lengths. Using the project photo as a guide, wrap two lengths around the box and one around the lid. Overlap the ends of each ribbon slightly, trim away the excess, and glue the entire length of each ribbon in place.

8 Using the heavy-duty jewelry glue, attach assorted costume jewelry, buttons, beads, ribbons, and rhinestones to the box and lid as desired.

Tip

- Stores sell decorative papers in various sizes. Often, packages of smaller sheets are available, as *collage* kits, for example. But some papers come only in large sheets. Even if your project calls for only a little of the paper, however, a large sheet is not a waste. Save the remaining paper for future projects.

MATERIALS AND TOOLS

Stamping tools and supplies (see pages 15–18)

Heat-embossing tools and supplies (see pages 11–13)

Stiff rectangular cardboard box with loose-fitting lid, about 7" wide, 9" long, and 5" deep

Medium-green mulberry paper, 25" x 36"

Beige mulberry paper, 25" x 36"

Olive green water-based dye-ink stamp pad

Embossing-ink stamp pad

Gold embossing powder

Assorted beads, buttons, bows, acrylic rhinestones, costume jewelry

Gold-colored ribbon, 3 yards long

Heavy-duty jewelry glue

Fern stamp (PSX, #F2585)

BASIC TECHNIQUES

Stamping (see pages 14–21)

Heat embossing (see pages 11–13)

Layering paper (see page 32)

Three-dimensional decorations (see page 35)

Sand Dollar Card

Feel the sand between your toes and the sea breeze against your face as you gaze on this subtle card, which features a combination of stenciling and dry embossing. A spray of raffia adds to the carefree, beachcombing effect. Why, you could just reach down and pick up that sand dollar right off the shore.

1 Tear a 3" square from the white vellum paper. Then dry emboss the sand dollar stencil in the center of the torn square.

Tips

- Raffia is a palm fiber that's been used for many years to make baskets and hats. Craft stores sell both dyed and undyed raffia. Crafters love raffia's versatility: You'll see it used in bows, braided wall hangings, handmade dolls, and more.
- For an optional seashore design, glue or stitch tiny seashells, fragments of driftwood, or even small beach pebbles to your card. As long as you plan to present the card in person rather than by mail, almost any lightweight, three-dimensional objects can be added as embellishments.

2 Before removing the stencil, use a stencil brush and the brown oil stick to apply color to the embossed portions of the paper.

3 Remove the stencil and lightly dry-brush the brown pigment onto the remaining portions of the sand dollar image.

4 Dampen the handmade paper and feather its edges by pulling them gently with your fingers.

5 Let the paper dry; then glue it to the upper portion of the card, as shown in the project photo.

6 Gather the strands of raffia, fold them in half, and position their folded ends on the handmade paper. Then glue the embossed vellum square onto the handmade paper, sandwiching the folded ends of the raffia between the two layers. Make sure the raffia is secure and trim off any excess.

MATERIALS AND TOOLS

Dry-embossing tools and supplies (see pages 7–9)

Stenciling tools and supplies (see pages 33–34)

Brown oil stick

Heavyweight white vellum paper, 5" x 5"

Lightweight handmade paper, natural color with flecks, 4" x 4½"

Parchment-colored ready-made card, 4¾" x 7"

Sand dollar stencil (American Traditional Stencils, #FS-915)

Several very narrow lengths of raffia, each 12" long

BASIC TECHNIQUES

Dry embossing (see pages 7–9)

Creating decorative edges (see page 31)

Stenciling (see pages 33–34)

Layering paper (see page 32)

Three-dimensional decorations (see page 35)

Holiday Ornaments

Some families have a tradition of making ornaments for one another as mementos of special holidays. As time passes, the ornament collection grows. Start your own family tradition with these fanciful, handmade ornaments, which will be cherished year after year.

White Ornament

1 Make a photocopy of figure 1 (see page 84), enlarging it to the dimension shown. To make a template for each of the ornaments, cut the pattern out.

2 Trace the outline of the template onto the back of the pale blue paper. Cut out the paper along the traced lines and crease the dotted fold lines.

3 Turn the pale blue paper face side up and place the border of stencil #MS-9 along one of the folds. Tape the stencil in place and dry emboss it using a stylus and light box. With the stencil still in place, use a stencil brush to fill in the pattern with the gold pigment ink. Remove the stencil.

4 Sprinkle the design with the gold embossing powder; heat emboss it. Repeat this process to create borders along all of the folds and straight edges of the cube. Embellish a small scrap of the pale blue paper in the same manner; you'll wrap this piece around the tassel. Set the papers aside.

5 Using stencil #BL-119, dry emboss a square motif onto the watercolor paper. With the stencil still in place, lightly dry brush the pattern with the gold ink. Remove the stencil and trim the paper close to the motif's edges. Repeat this process to create a total of six squares. Center and glue one square to each square surface of the ornament cutout.

6 Fold the ornament into a cube shape and glue the tabs in place. (Be sure to tuck the tabs under the square sections so they won't show when you're finished.)

7 Thread a needle with a 9"-long piece of the green embroidery floss and stitch it through one corner of the ornament. Remove the needle and let the ends of the floss trail from the ornament.

8 To make the tassel, wrap green embroidery floss around the 3" cardboard square 12 times. Carefully slide the looped floss from the board and attach it to the ornament by knotting the trailing thread ends around the loops on one end.

9 Trim the embellished piece of scrap paper to ½" x 1", wrap the scrap around the floss about ¼" from the knotted end, and glue it in place. Trim the floss to the desired length.

BASIC TECHNIQUES

Dry embossing (see pages 7–9)

Heat embossing (see pages 11–13)

Stamping (see pages 14–21)

Paste paper (see pages 22–29)

Folding (see "Tips," page 32)

Creating decorative edges (see page 31)

Three-dimensional decorations (see page 35)

MATERIALS AND TOOLS

Paste-paper tools, supplies, and recipes (see pages 23–25 and "Paste-Paper Ornament," step 1)

Heat-embossing tools and supplies (see pages 11–13)

Dry-embossing tools and supplies (see pages 7–9)

Stamping tools and supplies (see pages 15–18)

Pale blue art paper, 5" x 7"

White watercolor paper, 3" x 4"

Cardboard, 3" x 3"

Burgundy card stock, 5" x 7"

75-pound classic laid text paper: two sheets, 5" x 7" and 2" x 4"

Red card stock, 3" x 4"

Green, olive green, and turquoise acrylic paints

Gold metallic pigment-ink stamp pad

Gold embossing powder

Green, gold, and red embroidery floss

Green brush-tipped watercolor marker

Clear nylon thread

Victorian corner stencils (American Traditional Stencils, #BL-119, #MS-9)

Friendly Design Impressions star motif stamp (AMACO, Set #4)

Ripple-edge decorative scissors

Burgundy Ornament

1 Trace the outline of the ornament template onto the back of the burgundy card stock. Cut out the card stock along the traced lines and crease the fold lines.

2 Turn the card stock over, right side up. Using the gold metallic ink and the star stamp, center and stamp a star motif on each square section of the ornament. Stamp another star on a small scrap of the card stock.

3 Using the gold embossing powder, heat emboss the stamped designs.

4 Using the green marker, squiggle a few lines on the embossed surface of the card stock. Then spray the paper lightly with water and allow the marker ink to spread, creating a dark, mottled effect. Let the paper dry. Repeat this process if a deeper tone is desired.

5 Repeat steps 7 through 9 from the "White Ornament" instructions, using the green embroidery floss and the heat-embossed scrap of paper.

Paste-Paper Ornament

1 Using your favorite paste recipe and the classic laid text paper, prepare two sheets of paste paper. The papers shown were created with a cornstarch recipe. The artist who created them combed and brushed turquoise and green paints on the 5" x 7" sheet, and combed olive green paste on the smaller sheet. Let the papers dry.

2 Trace the outline of the ornament template onto the back of the 5" x 7" sheet of paste paper, cut out the pattern, and crease the fold lines.

3 Using a ruler and pencil, draw six 1" squares on the wrong side of the red card stock. Cut along the marked lines with the decorative-edge scissors. Cut six 3/4"-square pieces from the 2" x 4" sheet of paste paper. Center one of these on each red square and glue all of them in place.

4 Repeat steps 7 and 8 in the "White Ornament" instructions to create a tassel with red embroidery floss.

5 Cut a 3/8" x 1" piece of red paper with the decorative-edge scissors. Using regular scissors, cut a 1/2" x 1" strip of the primary paste paper. Center the red paper over the paste paper and glue it in place. Then cut a 1/4" x 1" strip of the second paste paper, center it on the red strip, and glue it in place. Wrap these layers around the floss about 1/4" from the knotted end. Trim the floss to the desired length.

Figure 1

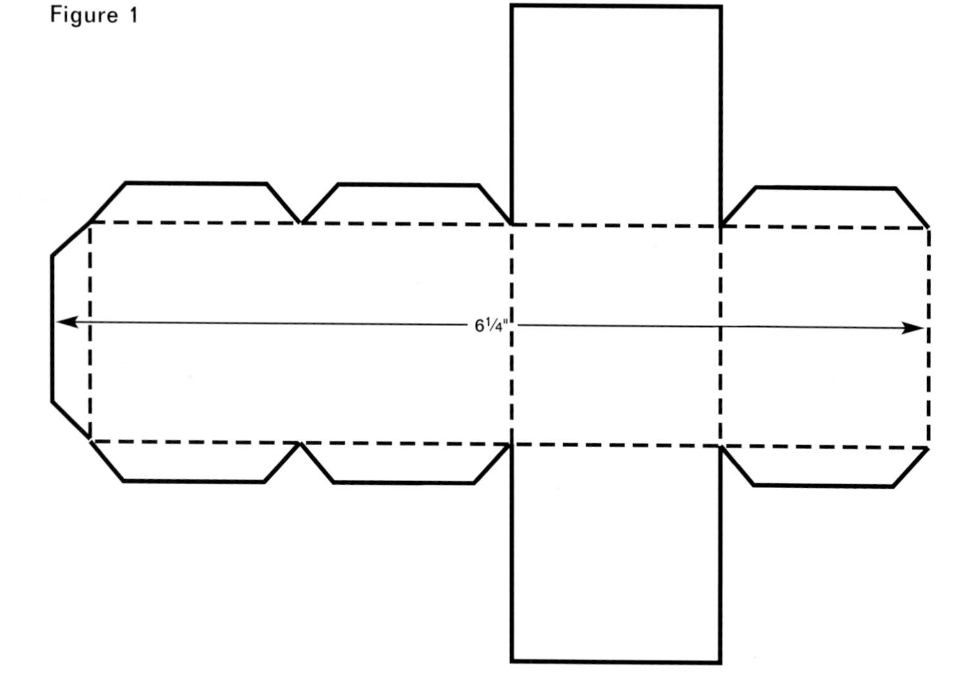

Tip

Use clear nylon thread to make an invisible loop from which to hang each ornament. Just use a sewing needle to stitch some thread through the corner that is opposite the embroidery-floss tassel and tie the thread off with a knot.

Desk Set

This desk set would make a beautiful graduation present, a welcome gift for a friend or colleague who is opening an office, or a special treat for anyone who treasures written correspondence. Choose a color scheme that will fit the recipient's decor.

MATERIALS AND TOOLS

Paste-paper tools, supplies, and recipes (see pages 23–25 and step 1)

75-pound classic laid text paper: three sheets, each 18" x 24"

Acrylic paints in coordinating colors

Granite-colored card stock, 18" x 24"

Granite-colored card stock, 15¾" x 21¾"

Granite-colored card stock, 6½" x 10"

Granite-colored card stock, 3¾" x 9¾"

Granite-colored card stock, 3½" x 9⅞"

Granite-colored card stock, 3⅞" x 9½"

Granite-colored card stock, 3" x 6"

Granite-colored card stock: two pieces, each 7" x 7"

Heavyweight cardboard, 16" x 22"

Heavyweight cardboard: two pieces, each 2½" x 16"

Heavyweight cardboard, 17" x 17"

Heavyweight cardboard, 4" x 10"

Medium-weight cardboard, 8" x 10"

Medium-weight cardboard: two pieces, each 8" x 8"

Leaf stamp (DeNami Design, #G83)

BASIC TECHNIQUES

Stamping (see pages 14–21)

Folding (see "Tips," page 32)

The Blotter Pad

1 Using the classic laid text paper, your favorite paste recipe, and acrylic paints, prepare three 18" x 24" sheets of paste paper and allow them to dry. The papers shown in the project photo were made from a cornstarch recipe. The olive-green paper was combed; the bright blue-green paper was brushed and combed; and the turquoise sheet was brushed and decorated with the leaf stamp.

2 To make the blotter, center the 18" x 24" piece of card stock over the 16" x 22" piece of cardboard. Glue it in place with craft glue or spray adhesive, folding the excess card stock to the back and gluing it down as well.

3 To make the two colored panels for the blotter, you'll cover two 2½" x 16" cardboard panels with paste-paper strips. Begin by cutting two 1¾" x 17¼" strips from each paste-paper sheet.

4 Position one paste-paper strip, right side up, over one long edge of a cardboard panel. Fold about ¼" of the paper under the panel's edge and glue the paper in place on the panel's front and back. (Let the paper's top and bottom ends extend beyond the panel; don't glue these ends down yet.)

5 On the front of the panel, mark a light pencil line down the glued paste-paper strip, ¾" from the panel's paper-covered edge. Take a coordinating strip of paste paper and fold over about ¼" of one long edge. Position the folded edge along the line you drew on the first strip of paper, aligning the strip vertically and horizontally with the first paper strip. Glue this second strip of paper in place. Prepare and position the third strip of paste paper in the same fashion, letting one long edge and the top and bottom ends extend beyond the panel.

6 Repeat steps 4 and 5 to cover the other 2½" x 16" cardboard panel.

7 Position the two panels, face up, at the two edges of the blotter. (Make sure that the card-stock-covered surface of the blotter is face up.) Align the exposed cardboard edges of the panels and blotter. Then fold the paste paper that extends beyond the edge of each panel around to the back of the blotter and glue the paper in place.

8 Center the 15¾" x 21¾" piece of card stock on the blotter's back and glue it in place to cover the paste-paper ends and edges.

The Letter Holder

1 Cut four rectangular pieces of coordinating paste paper as follows:

Color A: one 6½" x 18" piece
Color B: one 5" x 11" piece
Color C: one 6½" x 18" piece; and one 4" x 11" piece

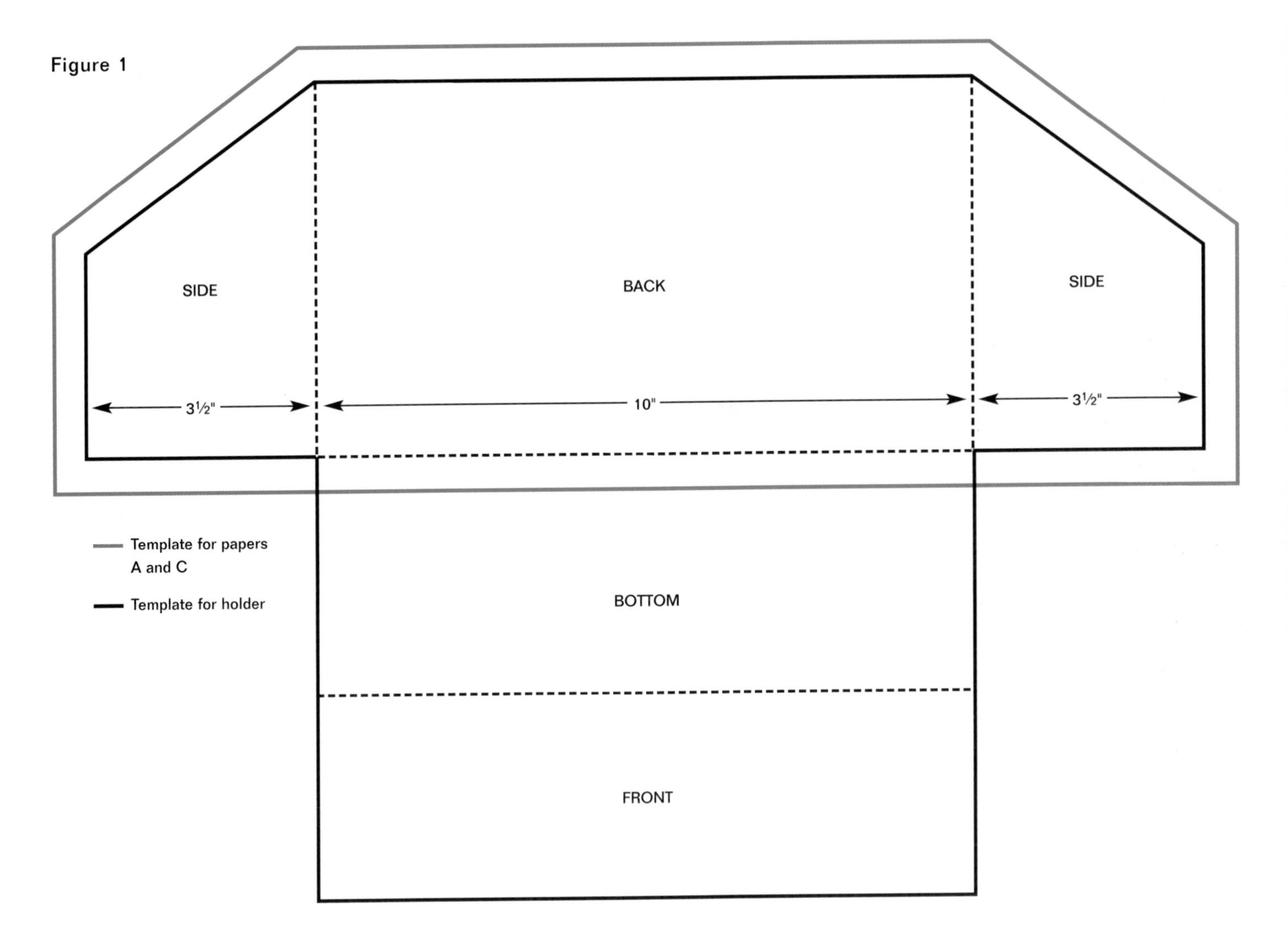

2 Make two photocopies of figure 1, enlarging them to the dimensions shown. From one, cut out the holder template; from the other, cut out the template for paper A and paper C.

3 Trace the pattern for the holder onto the 17" x 17" piece of cardboard. Cut out this cardboard piece. Trace the other pattern twice—once onto paper A and once onto the larger piece of paper C. Cut out these two pieces of paste paper.

4 Crease the cardboard holder at the dotted fold lines indicated on the pattern. Before assembling the holder, glue paper A onto what will be the interior back and interior sides of the holder, folding the paper edges over the edges of the cardboard.

5 To assemble the holder, fold the cardboard at the crease lines and tape the sides and bottom to hold them in place.

6 Glue the 4" x 11" piece of paper C onto the front face of the holder, overlapping the excess paper at the edges.

7 Cover the outer sides and back of the holder with the piece of paper C that you cut out in step 3, folding the paper under itself at the front edges and wrapping the other edges around the holder's edges.

8 Glue the 6½" x 10" piece of card stock to the inside front face and inside bottom of the holder, trimming it as necessary for a good fit.

9 Position the 4" x 10" piece of cardboard (the divider) inside the holder to check its fit. It should be just a bit loose. Trim it as necessary. Then glue the 5" x 11" piece of paper B over it, folding the paper edges over to the back. Center the 3¾" x 9¾" piece of card stock over the back of the divider and glue it in place.

10 Place the divider in the letter holder, with the paste-paper surface facing forward, approximately 1¾" from the back of the holder. Glue the divider along its edges to secure it.

11 Center and glue the 3½" x 9⅞" piece of card stock to the outside bottom of the holder.

Figure 2

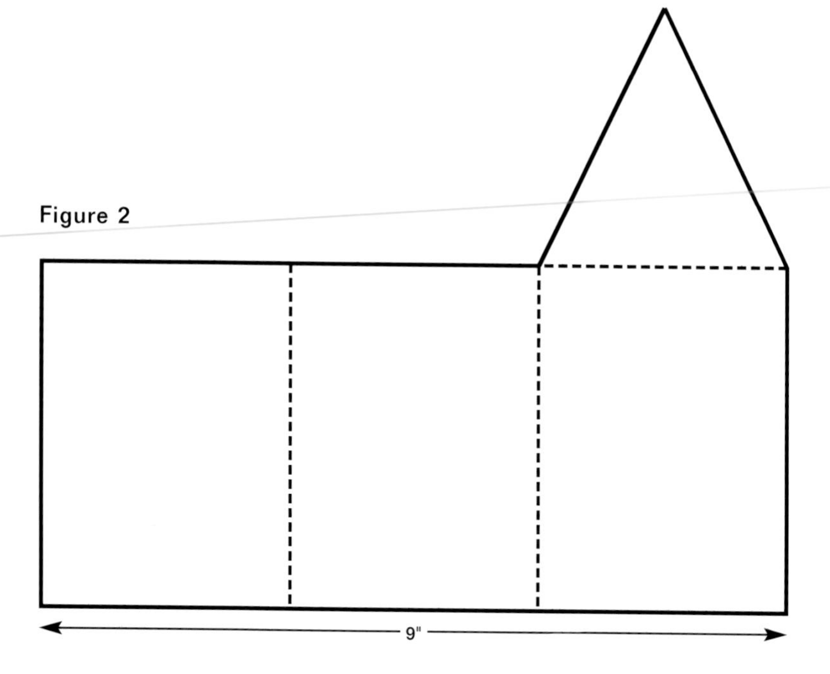

The Pencil Holder

1 Make a photocopy of figure 2, enlarging it to the dimension shown, and cut out the pattern along its exterior lines. Trace this pattern onto the 8" x 10" piece of cardboard and cut out the cardboard.

2 Crease the cardboard along the dotted fold lines indicated in the pattern; then tape the sides and bottom in place.

3 Cut out three pieces of coordinating paste paper, each measuring 3½" x 5". Position and glue one piece over one of the pencil holder's side panels, allowing ¼" of the paper to wrap around the panel's side and bottom edges and about ¾" to wrap over the top edge.

4 Position the second piece of paste paper over the next cardboard panel, but before gluing this paper in place, create a finished edge on the paper by folding over a ¼"-wide hem along the 5"-long edge that will overlap the previously glued paper.

5 Repeat step 4 to position the third piece of paste paper over the last panel, but before gluing it in place, fold both of its long edges back to provide finished edges.

6 Glue the 3⅞" x 9½" piece of card stock inside the holder to serve as a liner.

7 Using the base of the holder as a pattern, measure and mark two triangles on the 3" x 6" card stock. Cut these triangles out and trim each one to make it slightly smaller. Glue one triangle to the inside bottom of the holder and the other to the outside bottom.

The Notepad Holder

1 Make three photocopies of figure 3, opposite, enlarging them to the dimension shown. From one photocopy, cut out the template for the holder; from another, cut out the template for the liner; and from the third, cut out the template for the paste paper.

2 Trace the template for the holder onto one of the 8" x 8" pieces of cardboard and cut the cardboard out. Trace the template for the liner onto one of the 7" x 7" pieces of card stock and cut it out. Trace the final template onto paste paper and cut it out as well.

3 Crease the holder at the dotted fold lines indicated on the pattern and tape it together.

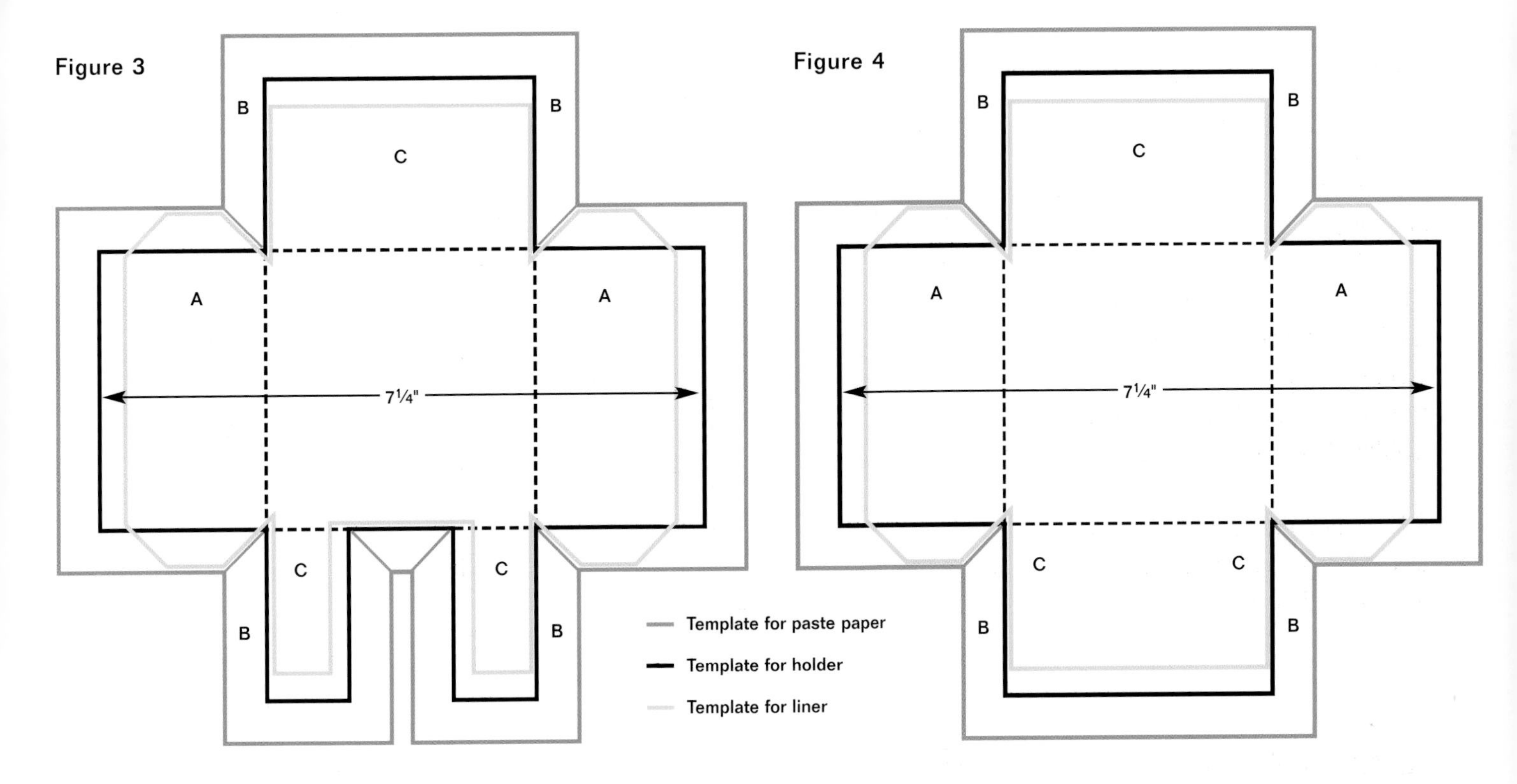

4 Place the paste-paper cutout face down on your work surface. Using the pattern as a guide, fold the B tabs inward. Place the holder on top of the paper. Then glue the paper A panels to the sides of the holder, folding their tabs over the top of the holder and around its sides.

5 Glue the three C panels to the holder, folding their unlabeled tabs to the inside of the holder. Their B tabs will provide finished edges on the holder's exterior.

6 Crease the card-stock liner at the dotted fold lines indicated in the pattern. Then center the liner in the holder and glue it down to cover the interior tabs.

The Paper-Clip Holder

1 Make three photocopies of figure 4, enlarging them to the dimension shown. From one photocopy, cut out the template for the holder; from another, cut out the template for the liner; and from the third, cut out the template for the paste paper.

2 Trace the template for the holder onto the remaining 8" x 8" piece of cardboard and cut the cardboard out. Trace the template for the liner onto the remaining 7" x 7" piece of card stock. Trace the final template onto paste paper and cut it out as well.

3 Crease the holder at the dotted fold lines indicated on the pattern and tape it together.

4 Place the paste-paper cutout face down on your work surface. Using the pattern as a guide, fold the B tabs inward. Place the holder on top of the paper. Then glue the paper A panels to the sides of the holder, folding their tabs over the top of the holder and around its sides.

5 Glue the two C panels to the holder, folding their unlabeled tabs over the top edges of the holder. Their B tabs will provide finished edges on the holder's exterior.

6 Crease the card-stock liner at the dotted fold lines indicated in the pattern. Then center the liner in the holder and glue it down to cover the interior tabs.

Stamped Clock

Make this beautiful clock to give to a special friend. The dazzling contrast of vivid colors against a black background makes it the height of modernity.

1 Using gold metallic ink, stamp the clock face onto the 4" x 4" black card stock. Cut out the stamped clock-face circle and set it aside.

2 Using the project photo as a guide, decorate the lower end of one of the larger sheets of black card stock by pressing the stamp pads with handles down on the paper to create three horizontal rows of squares (in lavender, orange, and parchment) and a solid inked bar (in lime green) above them.

Tip

- The clock shown in the project photo was made with some special items that are available at many craft and rubber-stamp stores. The first is a clock kit that includes the dial stamp, the clock mechanism, a hanger, and a 5" x 7" acrylic plate (with a pre-drilled hole) to serve as a base. You can make a similar clock from scratch and stamp any clock face on it, but use an acrylic base rather than thin card-board or wood, as those materials may warp over time. The other items are Option Plates—removable stamp pads with handles—but you may use any stamps you like to create a design of your own.

3 While the ink is still wet, press the uninked floral motif stamp onto the lime-green bar. The stamp will pick up some of the moist ink, and its image will remain where the ink has been removed.

4 Ink the floral motif stamp with evergreen ink and stamp four floral images onto the upper portion of the black card stock.

5 Place the black mulberry paper, right side down, on your work surface. Coat the back with spray adhesive and position the acrylic frame on top of it, centering the plate carefully. Turn the plate over and carefully smooth the paper onto its front face, leaving a 1½"-wide paper border all the way around. Use a craft knife to trim away a small circle of paper to reveal the hole in the plate. (Be careful not to leave grooves in the acrylic.) Then fold the paper border over the outer edges of the plate and glue it to the back of the acrylic plate.

6 Center the blank sheet of black card stock on the back of the acrylic plate. Trace the hole in the plate onto the card stock, and cut out the hole in the card stock. Then recenter the paper on the back of the plate and glue it in place.

7 Repeat step 6 to center the decorated card stock over the front of the clock's body and glue it in place.

8 Center the clock cutout over the decorated card stock on the front of the clock's body. Mark the area through which the clock mechanism will fit and cut a hole through the clock cutout in that area. Glue the cutout to the decorated card stock, aligning the holes in each. Then assemble the clock mechanism.

MATERIALS AND TOOLS

Stamping tools and supplies (see pages 15–18)

Clock kit (Magenta, #CLK-29.005.P)

Black card stock, 4" x 4"

Black card stock: two pieces, each 5" x 6¾"

Black mulberry paper, about 6" x 8⅛"

Gold metallic ink stamp pad

Floral motif stamp (Magenta, #14.211.F)

Lime green, evergreen, orange, parchment, and lavender pigment-ink stamp pads (Option Plates, Clearsnap; see "Tip")

BASIC TECHNIQUE

Stamping (see pages 14–21)

Embossed Frames

These beautifully embossed frames make a lovely pair. Their subtle shading and gently textured surfaces will enhance any pictures they surround.

Note: If you use the frame kit (see "Materials and Tools") rather than making a frame from scratch, omit steps 1, 6, 7, 12, and 13.

1 Using a pencil and ruler, mark a 3¼" square in the center of one piece of card stock. Cut out the square with a craft knife. The card stock should now be frame-shaped and about 1¾" wide all around.

2 Prepare the image to be stamped. To do this, soften a moldable foam stylus tip of your choice with heat from a light bulb. Then press the tip against the stamp wheel die to mold it into the pattern shown in the project photo. Let the tip cool and harden.

3 Ink the molded tip with the smoke-blue ink pad and stamp the design all over the card-stock frame. (If you don't have this special stylus, use the stamp wheel itself—or another stamp—to print repeated images all over the card stock.)

Tip

- The frames shown in the project photo were made from kits that are available at many craft and rubber-stamp stores (see "Materials and Tools"), but any commercial frame with flat surfaces to which paper can be glued will also work.

4 Using the clear embossing powder, heat emboss the stamped card stock. Let the surface cool.

5 Color the embossed card stock by applying the copper ink pad directly to it, making sure to remove any excess color with a tissue. Apply the clear embossing powder to the entire surface and heat emboss the surface once again. Let the card stock cool.

6 To make the frame, you'll cut openings in the four pieces of binder's board and then glue the boards together. Start by cutting a 3"-square opening in the center of one of the boards, to make a frame shape with 2"-wide borders. Cut 3½"-square openings in the other three boards, making sure that the holes are centered. (Save the cutouts.)

7 Stack and glue the frame boards together, placing the board with the 3"-square opening on top. Set the layered boards under heavy weights until the glue has dried completely.

8 Place the handmade paper, right side down, on your work surface. Coat the back with spray adhesive and position the frame on top of it, centering the frame carefully and making sure that the smaller opening in the frame is face down. Turn the frame over and carefully smooth the paper onto its front face, leaving a 1½"-wide paper border all the way around.

MATERIALS AND TOOLS

Stamping tools and supplies (see pages 15–18)

Heat-embossing tools and supplies (see pages 11–13)

Magenta frame kit #SPF or

- Light-colored card stock, 6¾"-square
- Binder's board: four pieces, each 7" x 7"
- Utility knife
- Heavy weights, such as books or bricks
- Lightweight beige handmade paper, 10" x 10"
- Window glass or acrylic, 3⅜" square
- Four swing clips (or turn buttons) and screws for frame back
- Picture-hanging clip and screw

ColorToolBox Stylus Tray (Clearsnap, #69004)

Country Border Rollagraph Stamp Wheel (Clearsnap, #964)

Smoke-blue pigment-ink stamp pad

Copper metallic pigment-ink stamp pad (raised or removable; see "Tip," page 91)

Clear embossing powder

BASIC TECHNIQUES

Heat embossing (see pages 11–13)

Stamping (see pages 14–21)

9 Using a craft knife, cut away the paper that covers the frame's opening, leaving interior borders of paper about 1" wide. Slice four diagonal slits in the four corners of the paper, from each inner corner to an inner corner of the frame.

10 Wrap the inner paper borders around the frame's inner edges and glue them in place, carefully smoothing down all surfaces with a bone folder, including the layered edges around the frame's opening. Then fold the outer paper border over the outer edges of the frame and glue them to the back of the frame.

11 Center the decorated card stock on the front of the frame and glue it in place.

12 Trim one of the 3½"-square binder's board cutouts (see step 6) to fit in the opening in the back of the frame. Cover it with handmade paper if you like.

13 Turn the frame face down. Fasten the picture-hanging clip to its back and insert a swing clip at each edge of the opening.

14 Place the glass in the larger frame opening, followed by the photograph you wish to display. Then insert the frame back and turn the clips to hold the assembled pieces in place. (If the photo is too loose in the frame, just place a thin square of cardboard between it and the binder's board square.)

Tips

- The designs on these frames were created with a special stylus (shop for this at your local craft or rubber-stamp store) that comes with removable, moldable tips. The tips are heated on a light bulb and then pressed against textured surfaces to create stamps and can be reheated and remolded repeatedly. If you don't have access to this tool, use any stamp you like to create a design of your own.
- If you can't find the frame kit and don't want to make the frame yourself, just purchase a flat, unfinished frame from a craft or frame store. Measure the front and back openings in it, and adapt the sizes of card stock (and the opening you cut in it); the handmade paper; and the window glass or acrylic. (This tip also applies to the project on pages 56–57.)

Acknowledgments

About the Authors

Susan Carroll is a freelance writer and editor with more than twenty years of experience in journalism. She was the managing editor of the award-winning Congressional Quarterly, Inc., book *Politics in America: 1996*. She left Washington, D.C., three years ago for the tranquillity of the North Carolina mountains, where she now pursues her interests in arts and crafts, gardening, cooking, and music of all kinds.

Barbara E. Swanson is a well-known designer with more than 300 of her original designs published to date, including patterns for cross-stitch, dolls, quilts, children's crafts, stenciling, and fabric painting. Numerous magazines and publishers have featured her designs, including *Better Homes and Gardens, Leisure Arts, Woman's Circle, McCall's, The Rubber Stamper, Arts & Crafts,* and *Quick & Easy Crafts*. Barbara also has several television appearances to her credit.

Contributing Designers

Sheree Y. Booth owns Blue Ridge Stamps in Swannanoa, N.C., and manufactured her own stamp designs for a number of years. She now teaches stamping to others and shares her passion for the craft with everyone. (Pages 6, 14, 30, and 35.)

Mollie Doctrow of Brevard, N.C., has been an artist and designer for more than fifteen years and teaches art at Brevard College. Her clients have included the North Carolina Wildlife Resources Commission and the University of California at Los Angeles, among others. She has received a number of grants, including a North Carolina regional artist grant. Her woodblock prints appear at the Folk Art Center in Asheville, N.C. (Page 68.)

Julie L. Klett, owner of Julie Klett Design in Portsmouth, N.H., has a bachelor of fine arts degree in oil painting and loves to tinker with creative things in her studio. She works with many media, including paper, fabric and fiber, ink, watercolor, and oil. Her creations have appeared in Portsmouth galleries. (Pages 54 and 80.)

Nancy Dunn Lawrence of Hayesville, N.C., grew up in Arkansas and recently retired from teaching elementary school. She enjoys bookmaking, writing, and paste-paper design; has taught marbling workshops for more than eight years; and has studied at the John C. Campbell Folk School in Brasstown, N.C. (Pages 27 and 28.)

Hélène Métivier, co-owner of Magenta Rubber Stamps in Mont Saint-Hilaire, Quebec, Canada, has worked with paper for many years. Her unique choice of colors and texture has rendered her works well known in the Canadian arts community. Her works have been exhibited in Vancouver, Toronto, and Montreal. (Pages 44, 56, 58, and 90.)

Kristi Pfeffer received her bachelor of fine arts degree from the Savannah College of Art and Design and has been a graphic designer at Design One in Asheville, N.C., for six years. She studied paste-paper design under Paulus Berensohn at the Penland School of Crafts in Penland, N.C. (Pages 22 and 27; her paste paper also is featured in Barbara Swanson's project on page 49 and Grace Taormina's project on page 70.)

Marie Philibert-Dubois of Magenta Rubber Stamps in Mont Saint-Hilaire, Quebec, Canada, is studying fabric design and transfers many of the techniques she learns to stamping and paper crafts. Her artwork reflects this in color and design. (Page 92.)

Louise Riddle of Weaverville, N.C., has been a professional art, craft, and floral designer for thirteen years, but she has practiced art techniques over the past forty years. The self-taught artist's first love is the expression of color, especially in nature. (Page 78.)

Mimi Schleicher of Weaverville, N.C., has been a full-time studio artist for more than a decade. She has two books and a videotape on marbling to her credit and specializes in designs for reproduction in industry. (Pages 22, 27, 28, 63, and 66; her paste paper also is featured in Barbara Swanson's projects on pages 82 and 85.)

Barbara E. Swanson, owner of Artistic Expressions in Marlborough, Conn., holds a bachelor's degree in clothing and textiles from the University of Connecticut. She has been a creative arts designer for ten years, and her work can be seen in consumer magazines, at industry trade shows, and in retail craft shops. (Pages 6; 30; 32; 35; 38; 49, also featuring Kristi Pfeffer's paste paper; 72; and pages 82 and 85, both also featuring Mimi Schleicher's paste papers.)

Grace Taormina is the vice president for product and creative development at Rubber Stampede, a manufacturer of rubber and foam stamps and accessories in Berkeley, Calif. She promotes the art of stamping through workshops and seminars at national trade and consumer shows. She also is a regular contributor of project ideas to magazines, books, and television shows. (Pages 42 and 70; the latter also features Kristi Pfeffer's paste paper.)

Nicole Tuggle of Asheville, N.C., uses a variety of paper-craft techniques to create unique cards and gift items. She uses her art as a means of communication, emotional release, and as a celebration of the simple act of giving. (Pages 6, 30, and 52.)

Virginia G. Turnbull of Brasstown, N.C., has been a professional weaver and spinner for twenty-four years. Her artistic pursuits include paper decoration, bookbinding, and restoration. She has taught classes in weaving, bookbinding, and paper marbling at the John C. Campbell Folk School in Brasstown and belongs to the Southern Highland Craft Guild. (Pages 22, 27, 31, 46, and 74.)

Emily Whittle of Red Springs, N.C., is a studio artist with twenty years of experience in the book arts. In addition to writing and illustrating children's books, she teaches workshops in bookbinding, calligraphy, and decorative paper techniques. (Page 60.)

Additional Thanks

This book wouldn't have been possible without the diligence and expertise of Lark Books Custom Publishing's **Chris Rich**, project manager; **Theresa Gwynn**, art and production director (who also contributed the handmade raised templates on pages 9 and 11); **Kim English**, project acquisition; **Skip Wade**, photo stylist; and **Amy Elizabeth Cook**, editorial assistant. For all the lovely pictures, thanks go to photographers **Evan Bracken** (Light Reflections, Hendersonville, N.C.) and **Richard Jolly-Hasselberg** (Jollyhassel Photography of Black Mountain, N.C.). Thanks to **Chris Bryant**, an art director at Lark Books, for his help with photo styling; to **Megan Kirby**, a designer for *FIBERARTS* magazine, for her terrific illustrations; and to **Coco Palmer** for letting us show her beautiful hands throughout the book. We also want to express our appreciation to several designers who went beyond the call of duty to review technical sections of the book and provide other invaluable assistance: **Sheree Y. Booth, Mimi Schleicher, Virginia Turnbull**, and **Emily Whittle**. We also thank **Jane Powell** and **Paul Aabye** of the Stamp Peddler in Saluda, N.C., and **Maryse Carrier** of Magenta Rubber Stamps for their help, as well as the knowledgeable staffs of **True Blue Art Supply & Services, Inc.**, in Asheville, N.C., and the **Michael's Arts and Crafts** store in Asheville.

Source List

Following is a list of the manufacturers whose stamps and other tools were either featured in the techniques chapters or were used to make the projects shown in this book. Some of these companies accept purchase orders from individuals. Others sell only to wholesalers; to purchase their products, visit your local craft store or rubber-stamp shop.

All Night Media, Inc.
P.O. Box 10607
San Raphael, CA 94912
www.allnightmedia.com
(Pages 27, 28, and 63.)
Wholesale only

American Art Clay Co., Inc. (AMACO)
4717 W. 16th St.
Indianapolis, IN 46222
www.amaco.com
(Pages 30 and 82.)

American Traditional Stencils
442 First New Hampshire Turnpike
Northwood, NH 03261
www.amtrad-stencil.com
(Pages 6, 7, 8, 9, 30, 34, 49, 80, and 82.)

Back Street, Inc.
3270 Summit Ridge Pkwy. NW
Duluth, GA 30096
(Pages 14 and 15.)
Wholesale only

Blue Ridge Stamps
450 U.S. Hwy. 70
Swannanoa, NC 28778
www.blueridgestamps.com
(Page 8.)

Clearsnap, Inc.
P.O. Box 98
Anacortes, WA 98221
www.clearsnap.com
(Pages 44, 58, 90, and 92.)
ColorToolBox™ Stylus Tray, Rollagraph® Roller Stamp System, Option Plate®

ClearStamp, LLC
(formerly Smiling Dog Designs)
2100 Roswell Rd., Suite 200C PMB 106
Marietta, GA 30062
www.clearstamp.com
(Page 15.)

DeNami Design
P.O. Box 5617
Kent, WA 98064
(Pages 6, 14, 15, 63, and 85.)

Heartfelt Impressions
2101 Welch Rd.
Kingsport, TN 37660
(Pages 14, 15, 19, and 21.)

Hero Arts Rubber Stamps, Inc.
1343 Powell St.
Emeryville, CA 94068
www.heroarts.com
(Pages 22, 27, 28, and 63.)
Wholesale only

Judi-Kins
17803 S. Harvard Blvd.
Gardena, CA 90248
www.judi-kins.com
(Page 63.)

Magenta Rubber Stamps
351 rue Blain
Mont Saint-Hilaire, Quebec J3H 3B4, Canada
(Pages 19, 20, 30, 44, 56, 58, 90, and 92.)
Wholesale only

Personal Stamp Exchange, Inc. (PSX)
360 Sutton Pl.
Santa Rosa, CA 95407
www.psxstamps.com
(Pages 6, 13, 14, 15, 21, and 78.)
Wholesale only

Rubber Stampede
P.O. Box 246
Berkeley, CA 94701
www.rubberstampede.com
(Pages 15, 19, 21, 23, 27, 28, 38, 42, 66, 70, and 72.)
Wholesale only

Stampendous!
1240 N. Red Gum St.
Anaheim, CA 92806
www.stampendous.com
(Page 15.)
Wholesale only
Designs © 1999 Stampendous, Inc., Rubber Stamps

Stampers Anonymous
20613 Center Ridge Rd.
Rocky River, Ohio 44116
www.stampersanonymous.com
(Page 15.)

Stamp Out Cute
7084 N. Cedar Ave.
Fresno, CA 93720
www.stampoutcute.com
(Page 15.)